Train Your Dog, Change Your Life

An Interactive Training Program for Individuals, Families, and Their Dogs

Maureen Ross, N.A., M.C.C
Gary Ross, M.E.

Hungry Minds™

Howell Book House
Hungry Minds, Inc.
New York, NY • Cleveland, OH • Indianapolis, IN

Howell Book House
Published by
Hungry Minds, Inc.
909 Third Avenue
New York, NY 10022
www.hungryminds.com

For general information on Hungry Minds' products and services, please contact our Customer Care Department within the U.S. at 800-762-2974, outside the U.S. at 317-572-3993 or fax 317-572-4002.

For sales inquiries and reseller information, including discounts, premi-um and bulk quantity sales, and foreign-language translations, please contact our Customer Care Department at 800-434-3422, fax 317-572-4002, or write to Hungry Minds, Inc., Attn: Customer Care Department, 10475 Crosspoint Boulevard, Indianapolis, IN 46256.

Library of Congress Cataloging-in-Publication Data

Ross, Maureen, 1953

    Train your dog, change your life: an interactive training program for individuals, families, and their dogs / Maureen Ross, Gary Ross.

    p. cm.

    ISBN 0-7645-6319-X

    1. Dogs—Training. I. Ross, Gary, 1954   II. Title.

SF431.R66 2001
636.7'0887—dc21   00-053839

Cover design by Michele Laseau
Interior design by George McKeon
Manufactured in the United States of America.

10 9 8 7 6 5 4 3 2 1

In memory of Kady ... our beloved Newfoundland, puppy trainer extraordinaire, cover dog, and therapy dog (for us as well as for others).

For all of our teachers, mentors, friends, and supporters.

Dedicated to Dorothy McAllister (Aunt Dot), a nature lover (dogs and horses) who continually inspires us with her wisdom, sense of humor, and grace!

Especially for our current pack: Elijah, Kelsey, Sage, and Casidy.

Contents

Foreword

Train Your Dog, Change Your Life is a welcome addition to the veritable pack of good dog books.

I can vividly remember the first time I met Gary and Maureen—sitting dead center in the front row of one of my behavior lectures in Boston. They always had something to say, Maureen especially, and now to the benefit of dogs and owners they have taken the time and trouble to put pen to paper. You'll find that their book is easy and enjoyable to read but above all, it's crammed full with oodles of useful tips and training techniques. Read and enjoy! Your dog will love you for it.

So many dog books fail to waver from the tired and well-worn, boilerplate formula and so from time to time, it's especially refreshing to read one that's original, interesting, challenging, and stimulating for the imagination. *Train Your Dog, Change Your Life* is just that—an utterly unique presentation of a wide variety of simple and effective dog-friendly (and family-friendly) training techniques.

To say *Train Your Dog, Change Your Life* is different would be an understatement. The book is completely different, eclectic to the extreme. Certainly in writing their book, the Rosses have drawn on the material of a wide variety of experts from many different disciplines within the behavioral sciences, but it's their inimitable blending, presentation, and application of the various approaches that makes their book as unique as it is useful. Indeed, the voices of many trainers and behavior counselors (for canines and humans) are echoed here—but what is especially delightful, from the viewpoint of dog lovers, dog owners, and dog trainers, is that the Rosses have distilled the essence of each view and suggested additional applications. For example, they encourage readers to consider that the human skills of listening and communication can extend to all aspects of one's life. Basically, *Train Your Dog, Change Your Life* comprises a wonderful compendium of the "the best of the best" plus a vast collection of creative, Rossian solutions to common dog problems, including house soiling, chewing, digging, barking, and jumping.

The Rosses have a passion for dogs and for education that springs from the text. Aside from this refreshing approach, the next best thing about their book is the emphasis. *Train Your Dog, Change Your Life* focuses on the very heart of dog training—relationships and interactions within the family, and awareness about yourself and in relation to your dog. Their philosophy is a simple one, but the best: Take time to savor life. Take time to enjoy yourself, your family, and your dog.

Their message is to consider that what we learn in the process of training our dogs—like making choices, taking responsibility for our choices, and discovering something new every day—can extend to other areas of our lives! It's about holding a mutual respect for all species. Before you can change your dog's behavior, you have to change your own behavior. This applies to any relationship with any species, whether human/dog, parent/child, partner/partner, spouse/spouse, and so on.

— **Ian Fraser Dunbar,** Ph.D., M.R.C.V.S.
Berkeley, Calif.

Acknowledgments

A guide, mentor, or coach is someone who recognizes potential in you as a person. Even though most mentors are busy themselves, they still take the time to share their experiences. They have mastered the art of listening and observing, which are the keys to understanding and wisdom. Without directly molding and shaping you, they are secure enough to put their egos aside for the moments they are with you. A good mentor will enlighten and inspire you. They always give you plenty of space to develop your own creative styles. They intuitively sense that there are some things that are just easier to do a certain way. So, they give you options and resources. They unthreateningly offer you advice and constructive criticism because they care. They want to make a difference. They are passionate about what they do. It's a delicate balance that they achieve.

The rest is up to us! We have the choice to remain at an impasse or we can reap the benefits of knowing that some things have previously been done well. We can learn from the experiences of these mentors, then integrate their teachings into our own creative repertoire, whatever that may be.

In this same vein, we need to be mindful of saying "thank you" and expressing our appreciation for the efforts of educators who create ways of making the complex and confusing seem understandable and useful. That's what it's all about. Learning is an eclectic accumulation of theories and paradigms enhanced by individual styles and techniques. We can carry the torch, in our own way, to make a difference in the lives of others.

Individually and together, we have and will meet many more mentors. Some have knocked our socks off with their ideas. They have greeted us with smiles and honored us with their wisdom, beliefs, and individualism. They radiate ways of creating positive change for people and dogs. Others, we prefer not to talk about. They are living in a very limited mind space.

We believe that our endeavors are the sum collection of these mentors. We have taken their ingredients and added some of our own to create a unique way of training dogs while changing your life and ours in the process.

We respectfully extend our heartfelt thanks to Dr. Ian Dunbar, who is an inspiration and pioneer for family systems and positive (food lure) training. You laugh and share mischief with us, while at the same time, continually show us that there is a different, and perhaps better, way of doing things.

Heartfelt thanks to all of the dogs, cats, horses, dolphins, birds, and other creatures that we have had the good fortune to learn from and share our lives with. What's next? We're ready.

Special thanks to our students, volunteers, and people in the community who have supported us from the get-go at Dog Talk® and TheraPet. You know who you are. Thank you to our families (biological and chosen) and friends who support us in our endeavors.

A warm thanks to Aunt Dot, a natural dog trainer and nature enthusiast, who shares a "knowing" that is true wisdom.

A big hug to Dr. Joan Cunningham who shares Trinity Farm, her wisdom, and studies of the behaviors of wolves, foxes, and any other creatures that join her "safe place."

We are grateful to our colleagues Terry Ryan, Karen Pryor, Turid Rugaas, Monique Charbonnier, Alan Bauman, Joel Walton, Wayne Hightower, Pam Reid, Jean Donaldson, and so many more. Tony Ziagos gives us an outlet to write every month at The Merrimack Journal. It's our pleasure to continue learning from all of you.

Appreciation to Dr. Jerilee Zezula at the University of New Hampshire who shares facilities, support, and expertise, enabling us to carry on with our passions, such as pet-assisted therapy.

Gratitude to the entire Leonard family who lend us their facility and unwavering support at a fraction of the cost that most people would request of us.

Cudos to Candy Dochstader, M.A., formerly of the Nashua Mediation Program in New Hampshire, for all her considerations on how to manage conflict gracefully, especially with families and aggressive behaviors!

Thanks to the Delta Society for providing a Standard and Practice for animal-assisted therapy.

Special thanks to Scott Prentzas and all the staff at Howell Book House and Hungry Minds, who are giving us the opportunity to express ourselves, while offering their expertise and creative advice.

Personally, we can't imagine our life without dogs. As Jeffrey Mouissaeiff Masson says, "Dogs never lie about love."

Introduction

Thank you for picking up *Train Your Dog, Change Your Life*. This book has evolved over a ten-year era while training families and dogs at Dog Talk®, our dog-training business. It's a collection of learning experiences harvested from the interaction, contribution, and feedback of our students, colleagues, friends, and, ultimately, the dogs.

Dog Talk has been an ongoing creation and accumulation of our passion for working with dogs and dog-related humans. It began in 1989 with a mission of offering gentle dog training. As we became wiser, it expanded to offer what we believe dog training is all about: awareness, education, and relationship-building skills. Many people were, and still are, disillusioned about dog training. Their expectations originate from past experiences and conditioning from family, friends, and society.

Training styles, reading materials, and tools run the gamut from being antiquated to barbaric to belly-roll laughable. Fortunately, we have recognized that there are better ways of learning and teaching, particularly when it comes to dogs and children. Every human and every dog is special with a variety of different capabilities.

With that in mind, Dog Talk began with the heartfelt intention to make a difference in the way we teach dog training. It germinated from the realization that we did not like or appreciate some of the styles of training we received with our own dogs. We sensed a need for change and embarked on a journey. Dog Talk was established with a mission to serve the needs of families, pet dog owners, veterinarians, and the community.

Our objective was to enhance human-canine relationships through awareness and education. This dogma is inclusive to all species. The objective remains the same today, complemented with the understanding that if we cannot change ourselves, the probability of shaping or changing our dog's behavior is implausible. By increasing our awareness and sensitivity about developing a relationship with another species, in this case canine, we can better understand ourselves.

Our goals are not lofty. We provide possibilities, alternatives, and resources to help people discover new ways of learning and making informed choices. Our passion is dogs. Our belief is that awareness, education, and developing relationships provide a gateway to expanding choices. These choices translate into new approaches that positively shape a dog's natural behaviors. It gives us the opportunity to explore different perspectives and develop broader interpretations.

ABOUT THIS BOOK

Train Your Dog, Change Your Life offers solutions for the prevention and modification of most common behavioral issues, which are usually no more than natural responses to previous consequences. All species do what works. We make choices, try out behaviors, and receive consequences. Based on our needs and desires to learn, gain gratification and attention, seek contentment, and survive, we decide what worked and do it again—not.

Training should be flexible, fun, fair, and forgiving, like a good relationship.

The buzzwords for training (and therapy, too) in this new millennium are *positive, interactive, solution-oriented,* and *cognitive-behavioral.* This book honestly shares our opinions about negative reinforcement, punishment, and the different results that can occur when they are used effectively (or not). We emphasize family-systems training as the most effective approach because it's our forte. Family-systems training is quick, reliable, and pleasurable for trainers, families, and dogs, but we realize it's not the be-all and end-all.

WHY THIS BOOK IS DIFFERENT

What makes *Train Your Dog, Change Your Life* different is that we have boldly dared to go where we think no one else has gone in a dog-training book. It's unique in that we have combined training, behavior, self-exploration, and self-help. It's not just about dog-training techniques. We ask you to take a close look at your lifestyle. What are your relationships like—not just with your dog, but with everyone? As Dr. Phil McGraw daringly shares in his book *Life Strategies,* "[W]e teach people how to treat us." We believe that we teach everyone, including our dogs, how to treat us. Chances are you are using the same patterns simultaneously in your life and relationships. Is there a pattern that you might like to change, or are they all working perfectly? Are you a recovering perfectionist and expect your dog to be, too? Do you procrastinate and wonder why very little gets accomplished? Do you dream about exercising and forget to take your dog for a walk?

Train Your Dog, Change Your Life will help you conquer two objectives at once and enjoy the process. While training your dog, you can begin to change negative or unhealthy patterns in your life, family, or relationships. It will help you manage your life and your dog in chorus. It's not an instant fix for mental and physical health, but it's a start. As the saying goes, pick up a mirror because we usually get the families, jobs, relationships, and dogs that we deserve. Many people prefer to stay in a comfort zone. It may not be a strong comfort zone, but it's a soft, safe place. If you can't change the way you think or do things, then you will remain stuck with yourself, students, clients, or any other impasses in your life. If mediocre is for you, great! If it's not, you must first acknowledge that change might be good. Get clear about what you want from yourself, your relationship (especially with your dogs), your life, and this book. The efforts you put into it will directly result in what you get out of it.

We strongly encourage you to join a positive-interactive training class, which should provide a safe environment that encourages people to observe, participate, and learn interdependently. It should be motivational and provide a springboard that catapults training from the classroom to the home environment. At home, you can use the self-help exercises, planner, and other suggested readings in this book to help you train your dog on a daily basis, while at the same time change the way you relate to yourself or to others. Your self-esteem will soar.

In that same vein, we have recognized that we can make a difference by getting people excited about taking charge of their training and their lives at home, not just in the classroom. A byproduct of a class is that people learn to communicate more effectively with each other and their dogs when they have a good instructor. It's impossible, however, to learn everything you need to know about dogs in a one- or two-hour training class for six or eight weeks.

A good training class should have a knowledgeable instructor with excellent handouts and leadership skills. Good instructors go over expectations, offer support, solutions, and request cooperation. They realize and acknowledge their own limitations. The instructors get people involved and encourage them to take accountability for their own progress. In this way, class time is maximized.

In our classes, we expect commitment because our perception is this: No matter what you're trying to accomplish in your life, once you're ready to learn the teacher will appear. You need to make up your mind that you can and will achieve success in training your dog, regardless of what kind of class you're in. You need to consider realistic and achievable goals that are conducive to success. Focus on your abilities, not on your flaws—or your dog's flaws.

TAKE A DEEP BREATH

Basically, people care about their dogs, sometimes more than the humans in their lives, and for good reason. Dogs listen and know how to play. They do not intentionally hurt us. More families are coming to our classes all the time, and, admittedly, it's not always easy for families or the instructors. Families can arrive tired and in a frenzy.

Rather than attempt to drum information through lecture and regimented hands-on training, we teach people how to breathe and relax from the get-go. We ask that they learn how to listen. (See "The Art of Listening and Observing" in Chapter Two.) Relax before beginning any training session or before issuing a corrective reprimand.

Taking a deep breath requires one second of your time and can make a world of difference in your attitude and reactive response. You have to breathe to stay alive anyway, so try focusing on it more often, particularly during stressful moments. The result is an amazingly calming effect on you, your dog, and the environment around you. We are 100 percent sure it will help you with clarity and making more effective spur-of-the-moment decisions that could affect your future training relationship with your dog. By beginning with a breathing exercise in the classroom, or at home, you will immediately notice a change in the ambience of the space you share with your dog. It becomes more serene. For some pups and dogs, it's the first relaxed moment they've had in a long time. In this peaceful moment of silence, the babbling stops, tension is released, people let go, and the pups lie down and relax.

From this vantage point, we encourage you to look at dog training and yourself through a wider lens (peripheral, like dogs), one that includes developing skills that will assist you in every part of your life. We don't just want to help you train your dog, we want to help you change the way you think about yourself in respect to training and your relationship with your dog. Call it therapeutic, if you like (because it is), but we feel that it's also about common sense and team effort.

We continually endeavor to develop classes that involve interdependence among dogs, families, and coaches (instructors). This book offers individuals and families alternatives and resources to be creative with, or not. Pretend we are your coaches. It's about choices. *Train Your Dog, Change Your Life* was designed to open up your mind to possibilities.

HOW TO USE THIS BOOK

This book is intended to accommodate different styles of learning: structured, unstructured, and blended. There is no right or wrong way, just different ways. We have some helpful tried-and-true suggestions to make it easier for you. We're sure about this: Knowledge has a profound impact on how we perceive things. It truly opens doors. What you do when you go through the door and the paths you choose to embark on are up to you. And, ignorance is not blissful. Rather, it's avoidance. It's a fear that there might be a better way. So use this book any way you want, but use it!

Some chapters are intended for you to read over and over again. Other segments are for specific issues, such as housetraining and barking. Structured lessons are in Section Two. Behavior shaping predicates that, like a chain, one needs to begin slowly to build solid, reliable links. Otherwise, a link will loosen, and the chain will fall apart. Not a good thing if you happen to be holding on to this chain for dear life in the middle of a walk in a high-traffic area with your dog.

Read up a bit on the basic behavior of dogs, shaping behaviors, body language, and most definitely Chapter Three, "Recognizing Canine Calming Signals." Learn a little about yourself and the role you play in building a relationship with your dog or with anyone else.

Complement the information in "Pawsitively Essential Exercises" in Chapter Five with the lessons in Chapters Six through Eleven, "The Six-Week Relationship Training Program." Progress through the lessons at the right pace for you, your family, and your puppy. As you read *Train Your Dog, Change Your Life*, you will satisfyingly discover that training takes place as part of your everyday living experiences.

Structured training sessions are required no more than two or three times a day for about 10 minutes. How much easier can it get? And, of course, you're aware that as life is on a continuum, so too is learning. Training never really stops, but it does get easier with practice. You won't even know you are doing it and neither will your dog. With practice, you will become so proficient at it that it will become a natural part of your day and life, just like taking a shower and brushing your teeth.

We encourage you to be imaginative, to giggle, and to develop your sense of humor. It's the most effective survival mechanism. Incorporate some of the suggested games, metaphors, and techniques with your own ideas to create an individual and original approach that best suits the needs of you, your family, and most of all the relationship with your dog.

Remember that you are the driver of your bus. You can think in or out of the box. You can go as slow or as fast as you like. You can sweat the small stuff, or not. You have alternatives and possibilities. Suggested readings are located at the back of this book, many of which expand on topics that you may choose to learn more about, such as clicker training, calming signals, or dog behavior.

Be in the present moment and reserve at least 30 minutes a day for yourself. (See "Personal Renewal for Dog Owners" in Chapter Seventeen.) Notice that the key word here is *yourself*. If you are all stressed out, unhealthy, and physically and emotionally out of shape, then what kinds of quality energy (relationship) can you offer anyone else? Allow your dogs to enlighten, encourage, and teach you how to live in the here and now. Dogs wake up everyday in the here and now. It's always a brand-new moment for them. They do not sit around all day with a laptop planning out their next escapade. Learn from this and enjoy the journey—it's a work in progress and you're responsible for the outcome. Remember, what happened in the past really happened in the now. What happens in the future will happen in the now. Therefore, the most important time for you and your dog is now. Learn from the past, plan for the future, but focus your positive energy now.

Children and dogs have always known naturally what adults can rediscover: Keep an open mind, play, laugh, smile, and learn something new every day. This is as easy and simple as opening the dictionary and picking out a new word on a daily basis. How long does that take while on your dog walk—a minute, maybe? Remember that your results will equal your efforts. For your efforts, especially with your dog, you will receive years of unconditional loyalty, love, and friendship with the species known as *Canis lupus familiaris*.

Please note that this book is a comprehensive guide but does not represent a complete understanding and/or program of behavior modification. As mentioned before, it's not designed to solve all of the mysteries of dog behavior or relationships. By all means, please seek out experienced counselors and educators. Ask your veterinarians for their advice and referrals.

Our quest is to empower you to keep an open mind and develop your intuition and sense of humor. Humor is a precious survival mechanism used by humans and other species since the beginning of time. You will read about how to use it carefully to de-stress and make training fun. Listen to your intuition. Take responsibility for your choices. Ask yourself what makes your heart sing. Learn to keep stress in perspective and use it effectively. Simply practice pushing an imaginary "pause" button and take a deep breath before reacting. A split-second reaction can leave a lasting impression, so try to make it a thoughtful one. By anticipating ahead of time what might happen, you are being proactive. Being proactive puts *you* in control, not the external stimuli.

Our intent is to get you stimulated and exhilarated about changing your interpretations about training and behavior, as it applies to all species and relationships in general. It can be scary and fun at the same time. Use these resources to help you easily integrate training into your everyday lifestyle. Positive-interactive training, effective techniques, and this book will bounce your training experience from the classroom to real-life situations.

Education and training is a lifelong learning process for all species. Enjoy the journey! Train smart, not hard. You will develop at least three valuable survival mechanisms: to breathe, to laugh, and to create change in your life. Are you ready to train your dog, change your life? Okay, then—take a deep breath, release, relax, and let's grow.

✦ ✦ ✦

"It's all but impossible to describe the new awareness that comes when words are abandoned. One is transported back, perhaps, to the world of early childhood, where everything is fresh and so much of it is wonderful. Words can enhance experience, but they can also take so much away. We see an insect and at once we abstract certain characteristics and classify it ... a fly! And in that very cognitive experience, part of the wonder is gone. Once we have labeled the things around us, we do not bother to look at them so carefully. Words are part of our rational selves, and to abandon them for awhile is to give freer reign to our intuitive selves."
—Dr. Jane Goodall, *Reason for Hope: A Spiritual Journey*

✦ ✦ ✦

Section One

Relationship-Training Fundamentals

Life without dogs, to us, is unimaginable. That's why we believe that dogs deserve at least the basics of shelter, safety, care, nutrition, exercise, training, and love. In this section, we will share with you years of experience, not just our own but also that of some dedicated people who spend their waking moments endeavoring to improve the bond between humans and dogs. These chapters will provide you with the fundamentals of relationship training — how to build a relationship with your canine companion that is based on teaching, trust, and respect.

There is always a moment during our interactions with dogs when a light seems to go on, and it is within that split second of illumination that we realize that training our dogs is more than just teaching them where and when to eliminate; what equipment to use; and supplying food, toys, and veterinary care. It is about bonding, awareness, education, and understanding another species — and developing a relationship.

We'll start in Chapter One with advice on how to puppy-proof your home to create a safe place for your new pup or older dog. In Chapter Two, you'll learn how to interpret canine body language, an important skill as you begin to train your dog. In Chapter Three, we'll introduce you to canine calming signals, another way for you to better understand your dog's behavior. In Chapter Four, you'll learn about behavior theory and discover that knowing more about canine behavior will help you get the desired results from your dog. This is going to be an exciting journey, so let's get started.

Enjoy the journey!

Chapter One

Creating a Safe Place

Puppy-proofing is only necessary as long as your dog is immature and in the process of learning house rules and boundaries. Puppyhood is the ideal time to teach these rules.

Puppies are curious and exuberant by nature. They are born investigators, seeking, searching, and finding anything that will amuse them. This behavior is part of the learning and discovery process. It's also a way to alleviate boredom and get some exercise.

HOW TO PROTECT YOUR PUPPY, YOUR HOUSE, AND YOUR SANITY

You teach! Create boundaries for your pup. Let's begin: Get down on your hands and knees. Crawl around your house and yard. Get a puppy's-eye view of the world. You need to see the world through a different set of lenses with a wider field of view. Be empathetic to your puppy's needs. Ask yourself, "What was it like beginning a new job, going to college, visiting a different country, or bringing home a new baby?" That is very similar to what a puppy, or an adopted older dog, experiences upon entering the new, human world—change.

Kitchen

Are you ready? Okay, let's crawl through the kitchen. Imagine what it was like, or would be like, having a toddler crawling around. Do you keep cleaners or chemicals under the sink? The contents of cupboards and trashcans can be wonderful exploration territories for puppies, but they're also very dangerous. Chocolate, for example, is toxic to dogs in large doses. Food and refuse in the trashcan (bones, cellophane, aluminum foil) can become lodged in the puppy's gastrointestinal tract.

Rotting foods, such as onions, can make a pup or dog very sick, requiring immediate emergency veterinary attention.

Make sure your cupboards are secured with childproof locks that cannot be pawed open. Keep closet doors shut tight (listen for the latch). Place chemicals and cleaners on higher ground, especially if you have a determined puppy.

Trashcans and garbage are enticing. The tantalizing wrappers and leftovers omit an aroma that's irresistible to the exploring pup's developing olfactory senses. Keep the trashcan secured in a locked cupboard. Use tight-fitting lids. Empty cans frequently, especially if you throw away meats, wrappers, cat food or fish cans, tins, and bones.

Family Rooms

Okay, let's crawl to the other living areas of your home. The TV, CD player, VCR, and assorted speakers have electrical wires and cords that are prime play targets for puppies. Bundle the wires and cords together using twist-ties, ropes, or rubber bands. Move them out of the puppy's reach. Tuck them behind the TV. Basically, move everything that you do not want explored to higher ground, at least temporarily.

There are some great sprays on the market that make objects unpalatable to puppies and dogs. Spraying furniture and other items can act as a deterrent. Be mindful that this will not prevent the pup from being toasted, should he choose to chomp down on a piece of wire. It's risky to leave this to chance and sprays. Prevention and supervision are the keys.

Temporarily move anything you treasure that's within reach to a secure place. This includes children's toys. Explain to children that the puppy could play with the toys and would probably chew them up. Let the kids know that the puppy will eventually learn to leave their toys alone, but right now he's in the process of learning the difference between his stuff and everyone else's.

Bedrooms, Bathrooms, and Dining Rooms

Baby gates are lifesavers. They will keep the puppy out of bedrooms and dining rooms. Close doors. Dirty laundry should be kept in hampers. Now crawl with me into the bathroom for a moment. Many owners will leave their puppies in the bathroom for short periods of time during the day. That's okay, but place all medications out of reach. Large amounts of acetaminophen and ibuprofen can be fatal. Small amounts can cause diarrhea, vomiting, and depression. Keep the toilet lids down, especially if you use drop-in tablets with chlorine or blue disinfectant!

Remember that puppies do not have a clue about the human environment. Scratching is scratching, whether it's in dirt or on expensive wallpaper. Unraveling toilet paper can be a fun and rewarding experience for your pup. Linoleum floors are great for teething. Bathroom rugs can be whipped all over kingdom come. Puppies can make chiffon pie out of your bath gels and soaps in a matter of minutes. Depending on how much havoc the pup creates in the bathroom, your repair bills could be costly. She may also ingest poisonous or harmful substances that could be lethal or require a visit to the vet. For short periods, it's a good idea to crate your puppy when you go out, even in the bathroom. Give the pup a few healthy, indestructible toys—Buster Cubes, Kongs, sterilized cow bones—to chew on.

Puppy-proofing measures, such as using gates to limit your new friend to specific areas, protect your puppy, your house, and your sanity. (Photo by Mary Bloom)

Let's crawl in reverse for a moment back to the bedroom and talk about crates. Allowing the puppy to stay in your bedroom at night is an optimal sleeping arrangement. The puppy feels safe being close to her humans. Usually, the pup will settle in serenely after only a couple of semi-sleepless nights. This can be in your bedroom or the children's bedroom. Establish guidelines by explaining to the children that the puppy should stay in the crate with the door closed. This will protect your belongings while preventing elimination accidents.

Garages and Basements

Another favorite place to accommodate puppies is the garage. What do you use the garage for? It can be a laundry room, and/or a storage area for yard fertilizers, pesticides, paint, thinners, antifreeze, glues, and craft supplies. These can be lethal if ingested. Antifreeze has a sweet smell that attracts puppies. Even a few small laps could kill a small puppy or dog. What else do you store in your garage? Potentially dangerous items are cardboard boxes packed with Christmas ornaments, tinsel, light bulbs, or heirlooms.

As we crawl through the basement, pay attention to furnaces, water heaters, and stored items. The safest way to leave a puppy in the basement is to fence off a reasonably sized area. This prevents the pup from damaging items or being harmed and gives you peace of mind.

Yards and Gardens

Now let's tour the yard and garden. Walk the length of your fence (if your property is so equipped). If you can't walk, then have someone else do it, or visualize all the things that can go wrong and make a list. Check for holes, loose boards, wires, gaps, or anything that might invite a puppy to explore, dig, or escape. Holes around fences should be filled in.

Dangerous debris (glass, lawn and yard tools, children's toys, lawn furniture) should be picked up, moved, and secured in a safe place. Check with friends who have successfully puppy-proofed their fence, or ask a fencing expert.

Do you have a pool or a pond in the backyard? Fence it off. Puppies and older dogs could drown if they haven't learned how to swim or cannot climb out. If you don't have a fence, section off an area of the yard. Build a safe run or a kennel for your dog with plenty of shade, shelter, and water, especially in the hot summer months. A dog's temperature can instantly rise in serious heat. Their normal temperature is from 101.5°–102.2°F. A dog can withstand a body temperature of 107°–108°F for only a very short period of time before suffering irreparable brain damage or even death. Heavy-coated and older dogs need special care and attention. They should *never* be left outside for indeterminate amounts of time without shelter and water in any season, particularly in winter or summer.

Remember that the growing pup needs exercise but should be supervised. Otherwise your dog could run away, be picked up by someone, get hit by a car, get shot, or drown in a pond.

Garden areas should be fenced off. Don't assume that your puppy will not chew anything because he hasn't before. Anything is a possible and tasty target. If you have questions about certain plants, ask your veterinarian.

Some Common Plants That Are Toxic to Dogs

Amaryllis (bulb), Avocado, Azalea, Boxwood, Buttercup, Cherry (pits), Chrysanthemums, Climbing Lily, Crown of Thorns, Daffodil (bulb), Daphnia, Delphinium, Dieffenbachia, Elephant Ear, English Ivy, Elderberry, Foxglove, Hemlock, Holly, Hyacinth (bulb), Hydrangea, Iris (bulb), Japanese Yew, Jasmine (berries) Laurel, Marigold, Marijuana, Mistletoe (berries), Mushrooms, Narcissus (bulb), Nightshade, Oleander, Peach, Philodendron, Poinsettia, Poison Ivy, Privet, Rhododendron, Rhubarb, Tulip (bulb), Walnut (nuts), Wisteria, and Yew.

In Case of Poisoning

If you suspect that your dog has ingested a poisonous substance, immediately contact your vet or the National Animal Poison Control Center at (888) 426-4435, or its 24-hour Emergency Hotline at (900) 680-0000. They charge a fee of $45.00 *per case*, which includes follow-up calls and consultation with your vet.

Puppy-Proofing Checklist

Use this checklist as a guide as you puppy-proof your home and yard.

These items should be removed, secured, or placed in an inaccessible area. This is not an exhaustive list. It mentions most items that a puppy can scout out. Use your imagination and good judgment.

Kitchen
- Cupboards
- Trashcans
- Food
- Breakables

Family Rooms
- Lamps and Tables
- Cords and Wires
- Televisions and VCRs
- Stereo and CDs
- Books and toys
- Knickknacks

Bedrooms, Bathrooms, and Dining Rooms
- Clothing, coats, shoes, underwear
- Furniture
- Toiletries
- Wallpaper
- Rugs
- Cushions and chair legs

Garages and Yards
- Chemicals
- Power tools
- Antifreeze
- Paint and paint thinners
- Pesticides and fertilizers
- Fencing
- Garden tools
- Lawn furniture
- Screenhouse

Chapter Two

Understanding Canine Body Language

We can't stress enough the importance of considering body language and attitude in relation to dogs. This chapter will familiarize you with the basic body language of dogs and show the effect of human body language in communicating with dogs, calming signals, and children and dogs. We'll look at how we can "inadvertently" teach behaviors that give us a headache later on.

Dogs communicate with body language and vocalization. The whines, barks, and howls translate into a meaningful message to the other pack members in the same way that we use our voices and body postures to express our emotions with family, friends, and coworkers.

Even though few of us are fluent in the fine art of dog language, and behaviors in a dog pack seem like foreign territory, most of us can tell the difference between a friendly and an unfriendly dog. It's easy to sense the aura of a confident and relaxed dog walking along with the tail wagging at an even height with the body. We have all giggled at the motorized twirl of a friendly Rottweiler or an Australian Shepherd stub.

Similarly, one can feel the tension emanating from a dog that's not friendly: His head is lowered, his ears are flattened with a glaring stare, his teeth are bared and growling. There may be a pilo-erection (hair stiff) along the back, straight taut legs, and a tail held high and usually vibrating.

It's difficult to live with a dog for even a few days without learning a wide vocabulary of his body language. Most of us know when our dogs are eager, sick, apathetic, depressed, or on the verge of some mischief.

Be mindful of your body language and attitude with respect to your dog. Use your body language and voice to suit the present moment. Less is better. If it seems out of context to you, then it's clearly out of focus to the dog. As you will recognize in the following pages, a little observation and conscientiousness about what children, the environment, and others can teach your puppy will make a world of difference.

✦ ✦ ✦

The good news is that the bad news can be turned into good news when you change your attitude.

✦ ✦ ✦

THE ART OF LISTENING AND OBSERVING

The art of listening at its simplest is taking in all that the other party is communicating. The art of observing is to see, watch, and note for scientific, official, or other specific purpose. It's to regard with attention to learn something. Put simply, listening reflects the art of being fully emotionally present without judgment or distraction. When we are fully present, we are not thinking about our work or worrying about how we are coming across. Our mind is free from judging ourself or the other being.

Similarly, while listening or observing, we are not formulating our response or considering our next move. Our thoughts are not stuck in the past or wandering to the future. We are fully open and receptive to what the other being is saying or doing, without having to change, fix, correct, or advise.

We listen, observe, train best, and "read" others' behaviors more accurately, when we are relaxed, centered, and have a sense of inner peace, well-being, and a good sense of humor.

Therefore, the art of listening and observing is species-inclusive. It's inextricably linked to the art of quieting and centering dogs and ourselves. Listening can be considered both an art and an active sport. Both require practice whether the intended use is for humans or for dogs.

Active Listening

We can all improve our capacity to listen, and it's well worth the effort. Listening well is at the heart of intimacy and the connection that leads to a healthy relationship. When we are able to listen to another person (or species) with attention and care, that being will feel validated and the relationship enhanced. With our dogs this can be defined as observing body language, listening to their vocalizations—whining, growling, or barking—and being aware of their responses to our requests and/or expectations.

The following skills that enhance effective communication may sound obvious, but they bear repeating and conscious practice on your part until they become second nature.

What's this Pomeranian saying to you? Learning the basic body language of dogs is important to building a strong relationship with your pet. (Photo by Winter-Churchill Photography)

Restating

→ **For Humans:** Repeating, word-for-word, a short statement or phrase the person has made.

→ **For Dogs:** A similar gesture would be redoing a training exercise to observe what's going on. Is the dog making mistakes or responding correctly? If not, you need to take a step back to observe yourself and the dog. What is happening with the communication? Is there a barrier that's preventing you from communicating your message of, for example, "sit" in a different location? Have you taken your dog to any new locations besides the home or training class? Have you tried requesting a "sit" or "down" with your back turned to assess whether your dog spatially knows what the word means? Maybe it's time to expand your repertoire; give yourself and your dog a challenge.

Listen to what you communicate to your dog. Observe what your facial expressions and body language say. Instead of "No, no, no" when your dog joyfully jumps up, try teaching "off" and "sit." Be specific and be positive. Teach what you want. Put behavior like barking on cue before the behaviors become a nuisance. Always reward "quiet."

Paraphrasing

→ **For Humans:** Recounting, in your own words, a short statement the person has made.

→ **For Dogs:** Recounting, *with your own interpretations*, why you *think* the dog is doing a particular behavior. Break it down. Try modifying your requests. For example: Try putting your hands in your pockets if your dog is anticipating the "come" when called. Use your voice only. Very often the dog is responding to a different cue. If it's an unwanted behavior, change the basic stimulus. For example, if your dog is all over you when you walk through the door, change the sequence. Teach your dog that he has to go get his favorite toy before you will greet him. This is easy, and your dog will be highly motivated. After all, the reward is you.

Are You a Good Listener?

Does it bother you when someone interrupts you? Interruption tends to bother good listeners. There are exceptions to this rule as some people interrupt nonstop. What this refers to is normal conversations at work, with family, and with friends. Is it difficult for you to listen until they finish a normal thought of communication without beginning to formulate your response? Ask a trusting companion (your dog perhaps), a friend, or a colleague. Be honest with yourself in this assessment. We have all been poor listeners at one time or another. The only way to improve is with practice.

Another way of assessing how well you listen to any species is the talk-to-listen ratio. Do you talk more than you listen? Next time you have a conversation, take a deep breath and pause before adding your two cents. When in doubt, ask. It's perfectly acceptable and admirable to ask someone, "Am I talking too fast, too slow, or saying too much?" With your dog, offer an "I'm sorry, that wasn't good enough, let's try again."

A greeting ritual among dogs is very much like the greeting humans receive from dogs that are not taught to sit before greeting. It's quite natural for dogs to greet other dogs by jumping, sniffing, and pawing each other's faces. They arc to each other's sides, sniff body parts, and sometimes pyramid one another in the attempt to establish who they are in the hierarchy.

Dogs get exhilarated at the very thought of being around their humans if the experience has for the most part been a positive one. This can be misinterpreted by some owners who do not listen, that is, do not consider the how, what, when, and where these behaviors emerge. Has the dog been cooped up all day? If so, they are ecstatic to see you. Have they eaten or had any quality time or exercise? Have they been to train-ing class and socialized to a variety of sights, sounds, and smells as often as possible? Essentially, have they been taught how to greet you as a human, and not as a dog?

Integrate training into everyday life. Teach "sit" before greeting, feeding, going down a flight of stairs, passing through doorways, before getting into the car, and going outside. Observe your dog's behavior to catch that threshold that most dogs cross from playing to being obnox-ious. Ground them with a "sit" or "come here" before they go too far. If you watch your dog, you should be able to recognize these thresholds. Our American Bulldog, Casidy, displays them particularly when com-municating. She does the usual greeting ritual, sniffing, side-by-side interaction, and then she playbows, looking for a response. If she gets an inkling of one that says, "Okay, let's play" from the other dog or person, she's off like the Energizer bunny. The more excited she gets, the more difficult it is to calm her down. What do we do? Lots of "jolly-ups and settle-downs" (see Chapter Five, "Basic Training For Puppies"), so she knows when we say, "Okay, that's enough ... sit," she should and does. She has learned the difference, and we are very aware of noticing that "turn-on point" in her behavior. Therefore, we can manage it. So can you if you become a dog watcher. Know what your dog's idiosyncrasies are, then you can manage them before they cross over to the dark side.

✦ ✦ ✦

Tension is who you think you should be...

Relaxation is who you are.

✦ ✦ ✦

All species develop defense mechanisms at different levels. For humans, this is purely psychological. For dogs, it is for survival in a human world.

We all suffer from the "yeah, buts": *Yeah, I know, but at home he always sits. I don't understand why on our walks at the park she won't sit. She likes children, but growled at my husband Rick and the UPS man. I have been planning on attending a training class, but I don't have the time. I've been meaning to teach my dog not to jump on people, but it's just way easier to put him in his crate or on a cable outdoors.*

Do any of these sound familiar? We all have excuses and busy lifestyles. Nothing takes the place of teaching a dog what you expect from the get-go (as early as eight weeks old). Puppies begin learning on the day they are born. Train early and learn to listen to your instructors and veterinarians. Ask questions. We can't all be experts at everything, but plenty of information and valuable resources are available for all of us. Be wise, process the information, and use what intuitively feels true for you and your dog.

We have all experienced butterflies and nervousness, perhaps before giving a presentation or meeting new in-laws. Sometimes we have an energy drag where we are just too tired or weak to listen. As mentioned previously, being stressed out is not a positive mindset for good listening or training.

Poor listening can also be a habit acquired from generation to generation. Do you remember feeling heard as a child, adolescent, or adult within your family system? How about with friends? Can you get a word in edgewise? Sometimes people don't listen because they have low expectations. They assume that the person or dog communicating doesn't have anything to contribute. Some have low self-confidence or self-esteem, thinking that what they have to say is of little importance, so they just keep talking. Then, they do not have to risk hearing what others say.

Hearing Aids

Here are some simple, easy tips to help you break down barriers of communication and learn to listen and observe humans and dogs.

First, you need to clear away the clutter and excess baggage (your old notions). Imagine you have a "pause button" in your head. Quieting your mind, taking-a-deep-breath, and pushing your pause button (count "one, two, three, four, five") will help relieve tension and awaken your senses. Dogs do not need to hear chitchat and constant blabbering. They live in the present, a lesson that we humans should cherish.

Second, wake yourself up. Act and look the part of an alert, good listener. Whether you are training your dog or giving a presentation, be prepared; know your material and/or act like you do. Sit or stand up straight, lean forward, uncross your legs and arms; get your blood flowing. Use appropriate eye contact and show interest, even if you have to pretend. Pretending can sometimes bring you into the reality of learning from the experience.

Communication Skills and Body Language

Along with good listening, communication skills embody a delightful combination of observing body language while sending, receiving, and processing information in a format that's meaningfully understood to that person or species. Accompanying this are interpretations, perceptions, and individual perspectives.

Engage your dog in conversation while training, walking, exercising, and playing, but do so while you are conscious of it. Take a moment and giggle here if you like, but most of us have to admit that we can go through half a day, and occasionally weeks, in a daze.

If you are training your dog this way, she will let you know with her lackadaisical attitudes and responses. Dogs are good barometers of our own behavior. If we are numb, they'll give a numb reaction. Be present and observe your dog's body language and response to you.

Here are some helpful skills to integrate into your daily communication with yourself, other humans, or your dogs.

• **Verbal and nonverbal cues:** Watch for eye contact (how long, averted, direct; see Chapter Three, "Recognizing Canine Calming Signals," for more details and illustrations). Look for signs of stress: yawning, licking, panting, and confusion. Be mindful of spatial cues from either dogs or humans. For some dogs (especially ones you don't know), the saying goes: "You stand there, and I'll stand here, but please don't get in my face." This is about culture and giving people or dogs appropriate space. As it can be offensive to some people to talk straight into their faces, or too closely, it's a no-no for either another dog or human to dash straight on into a dog's face. A side or diagonal approach is less threatening and gives you both the space required while assessing the next move.

• **Ferret out boredom:** Look for yawning, napping, disinterest, and making "perceived" mistakes. If you, your dog, or another person does any of these behaviors, the message is clear: The situation is going downhill; there is disinterest and boredom.

• **Encourage the flow of communication** between you and your dog. The communication is broad in nature and most of the time non-threatening if you learn how to observe a dog's body language (see the body-language illustrations later in this chapter).

• **Train in short segments:** You'll get better, more reliable results from 10-minute sessions, held two or three times a day, than from one long, drawn-out, boring 30-minute soliloquy.

• **Probe:** Probing is a fun and thorough way of gathering specific information to enable you to easily highlight areas that need improvement in training. Simply spotlight situations that happen by making a mental note, or preferably, by writing it down. Ask yourself direct questions: "What do I want to change about or teach my dog? What behaviors bother me the most? What have I done in the past? Was it successful? Did it make the behavior worse? Are my interventions prompt (timing)? What's my dog's lifestyle like? Has anything changed in my lifestyle lately (death, divorce, new baby) that might be affecting my dog's behavior? When does Fraser usually run away? What's happening? Where does he run to and what do I do when he returns? Who administers correction and in what ways?"

• **Interpretation:** As previously mentioned, 10 behaviors equal 10 interpretations. "I wonder if my dog Ian eliminated in the house because he hadn't been out for several hours?" This is a nonthreatening assumption that gives you the opportunity to be proactive rather than reactive.

• **Confrontation:** Watch for nonverbal cues from your dog. "I have no idea why Sabrina runs away from me, but I recall that in the past I have used physical punishment and a strong, verbal reprimand when she returns." Confronting a returning dog is a counteractive conditioning action. Would you approach someone who had screamed at you, then socked you in the face?

- **Reframing:** Each human and dog has his or her own picture of a situation. If the picture doesn't change, there is no reason for a dog to react or behave differently. Dogs build a catalog of do's and don'ts in their brains. They "guess" to survive. It's either pleasurable or not, safe or dangerous. One way of reframing is to find the positive in a negative situation. Reflect back on what you want. What are your goals and expectations? Is it achievable for you and your dog? Are you going too fast, too slow? Focus on skill building one step at a time. Make it fun, fair, flexible, and forgiving.

- **Snapshot small successes to meet training goals:** A small step is far better than a big failure.

Listening and communicating comes in various cultures, styles, and forms. It truly is an art that with practice can enhance your relationship in just about any situation. If you've been using the same techniques for years and you're miserable, then it's time to try something new. Be aware and consciously in the moment. Take some time every day to be aware and practice new listening and communication techniques with friends, families, business cohorts, and your dogs. Become a professional flirt, knowing how to get people and your dog to do what you want in a savvy way. Praise and compliments colored with integrity, fairness, and honesty work wonders.

Classic Example

<u>Human:</u> "Casey is impossible. He urinates in the house, chews the couch, and I know he does this to hurt my feelings. He is mad at me ... boohoo, boohoo, boohoo."

<u>Reframe:</u> "Casey is doing some behavior that is unacceptable to me. I need to work on teaching Casey where to urinate, what to chew, and I need to learn more about how dogs communicate with humans. I wonder if I'm giving him too much space in the daytime. Maybe I should confine him in a crate with a couple of good chew toys. I know he's only doing this because he's confused. I need to go back to training class. I need some support. We both need more exercise."

DOG EMOTIONS

One of the best books describing the emotions of dogs is Dr. Jeffrey Moussaieff Masson's *Dogs Never Lie About Love.* Dogs do have emotions, but not in the same way as humans. They do reason and learn. Dog trainer Kathy DeLong emphasizes, "If dogs didn't have emotions or reason, then how could a guiding-eye dog who is trained to 'see' for humans know when to force its human, against a direct command to go forward, to stay on the curb, because a Mack truck is going to run them over?" Some may conclude that this is purely self-preservation. The dog doesn't want to get killed, therefore, he urges his owner to stay put. This may be true, but what difference does it make? The point is that in the process of saving their own rear-ends, dogs will save ours, too.

Dogs don't premeditate. They just do what they do and do it again, or not, depending on the consequences. Their emotions are pure and intense. What you see is what you get. They express themselves with zest when they are happy and pout with a passion, letting us know when they are sad. Their body language, if you take the time to read it, clearly expresses confusion, fear, anxiety, enthusiasm, joy, or playfulness. Therefore, it behooves all of us to respect a dog's movements, body language, and signals and/or emotions (whatever you prefer to call it).

Turid Rugaas has articulated the various signals of dogs in her book *On Talking Terms with Dogs: Calming Signals.* Behaviorists and trainers use her studies worldwide. Calming signals are a universal language used to maintain a healthy social hierarchy and resolution of conflict within a pack. These are skills that, when carried over to our own interaction with dogs, can be highly beneficial to our relationship. Dogs have the instinctive ability to calm themselves and others in the face of stress or fear.

✦ ✦ ✦

"The effect upon the dog of his life with Man is discernible in his eyes, which frequently are capable of a greater range of expression than Man's. The eyes of the sensitive French Poodle, for example, can shine with such an unalloyed glee and darken with so profound a gravity as to disconcert the masters of the earth, who have lost the key to so many of the simpler magics. Man has practiced for such a long time to mask his feelings and to regiment his emotions that some basic quality of naturalness has gone out of both his gaiety and his

solemnity. The dog is aware of this, I think. You can see it in his eyes sometimes when he lies and looks at you with a long, rueful gaze." —James Thurber

✦ ✦ ✦

GROWLING

Growling is a valuable behavior for dogs. Our experience is that growling is one of the most misunderstood dog behaviors for our clients. We all know that dogs need to dig, chew, chase, eat, pee, poop, run, play, and bark. It's their nature. It follows that growling is very much a part of their nature as well.

Growling can be considered an ambiguous behavior. That is, it isn't always clear what our dogs are telling us when they growl. (The best summary we've found on growling and other ambiguous behaviors is an article written by Dr. Ian Dunbar titled "Ambiguous Behaviors.") Dogs growl for any number of reasons. They can be reacting to a threat, scared, frustrated, exhibiting a lack of confidence, using it as a form of learned helplessness, or even just playing.

Growling is divided into three levels: The first is play, the second is fear-based, and the third is used as a warning prior to aggression. Growling is used, when integrated with the dog's other behaviors, to communicate how he feels and what his intentions are. Think of ourselves in the morning before our first cup of coffee. Have we been known to "growl"? Are we, as "educated observers of the human condition," aware of each other's relative state of mind? The answer is: "Probably so." We know from experience to stay away from Fred until he's had his coffee. How do we know that? We watch and listen. We integrate the whole body picture. Dogs do the same thing, except they have an added advantage in that they have their acute sense of smell and a wide-angle lens working for them as well. Growling is one part of the puzzle that, if taken by itself, can be easily misconstrued.

Look at the Big Picture

What should you do if your dog is growling? First, try to determine what he is growling about. Is it play? What's the tail doing? Is it high or low? Wagging? How fast? What are the ears doing? Are they pricked up or laid back? Where is the dog? Has this happened before? With children perhaps? How many times, where, when, with whom, and what did you do? What were the results? Record this information for future reference, particularly if growling is something you're trying to understand.

Refer back to the body-language illustrations in this chapter, as well as to Chapter Three, "Recognizing Canine Calming Signals." Calmly ask the dog, "How are you feeling?" Try a simple command to take control of the situation back from the dog. Change the subject. Call him to you and have him "sit." Have him do another simple behavior, e.g. "down," "paw," "speak," whatever. Remain neutral. If you can get control back, then you're OK. Chances are the dog has even stopped growling. Then try to figure out what's bothering him.

Never punish the dog for growling. Growling is the dog's "early-warning system." Punishing this behavior can result in its elimination from your dog's repertoire and can be a huge disadvantage for you. The only time that one of us was bitten by a client's dog that was conditioned by his previous owner not to growl.

It must be noted that the frequency and amount of vocalizing seems to be an individual thing. Clearly some breeds growl more than others. Rotties are famous growlers. Our Newfies play-growl like bears. That's OK, but we need to remember that to many people, perception is sometimes more important than reality. Any growl is a bad growl to a lot of folks.

Grounding

Back to the three levels of growling. The first level is play-growling, which manifests itself during roughhousing, such as wrestling or tug-of-war. Note that these behaviors are not species-exclusive; i.e., they can occur dog-to-dog or dog-to-people (or people-to-people for that matter). These growls express pleasure and are not a matter for concern. However, care must be taken to ensure that the play remains grounded and doesn't escalate into one of the next two levels. Being grounded refers to keeping the play under control by periodically throwing in a request for a behavior, e.g., "Sit, give ... OK, take it!"

The second level of growling is a growl based on fear. Again, please refer to the body-language illustrations in this chapter, as well as to Chapter Three, "Recognizing Canine Calming Signals." This is the dog's attempt to tell another creature, "Back off, you're making me nervous or scared." Generally speaking, fearful growling starts fairly late in the back-off game. If we understand posture and calming signals, then there should be ample other warnings that the dog is uncomfortable before they growl.

The third type of growling is that which comes prior to aggression. It's interesting to note that, for the most part, the growliest dogs are not the top-ranking dog but rather middle-ranking types looking to make their way to the top. They can be blustery. The top-ranked dogs, being secure in their place, don't see the need. As a wise person once said, "Those who can, do. Those who can't, talk about it." Most of us wait far too long. The response to this kind of activity is the same as above: Change the subject and take back control.

Owner-Animal Relationship

Let's think for a moment about those things that might prompt a growling session between an owner and his or her dog. Let's start by examining our own relationship with our dog. Is it based upon mutual understanding? Or is it based upon fear ("Do what I say or else...")? Too many training methods over the years have relied on our interpretation of how dogs interact. Specifically they imply that physical domination is necessary in order to have a good dog. We disagree 150 percent, especially for a family dog. Techniques such as the so-called Alpha Rollover (rolling your dog over onto his back to establish dominance) not only can be damaging to your relationship with your dog, but can also be physically dangerous. Amongst dogs (or wolves—their ancestors), the subordinate dog rolls over on her own; she isn't forced there. Do not delude yourself into thinking that the dog thinks you are a dog or an alpha wolf. She knows you're not and is probably chuckling at the thought.

So what does this mean to the dog? Simply that you're being cruel. A true alpha dog will dominate the lesser members of the pack mentally, not through physical domination unless absolutely necessary. What the alpha dog does usually happens quickly and sometimes too fast for the human eye.

Unfortunately, if you are using methods based upon domination and your dog tries to divert or express his concerns by freezing, cowering, or running away, chances are he will suffer further physical punishment. This is clearly their sign to you that he gets the message. He is acquiescing. So, ask yourself, is this the kind of relationship you want to have with your dog? We hope not. The special relationship between dog and human is too precious to waste with our own insecurities or needs to be the boss. And, when it comes to educational material, there is plenty of it, but be picky and choosy. If it sounds and feels right to you, then it probably is. Listen to your intuition. Train your dog. Learn from each other. Expand your relationship. Seek out knowledge. Have fun. Because if you both have fun and understand the growlies of the first kind, chances are that your dog will not feel the need to escalate his growls to the second and third kinds.

Our experience, after doing hundreds of assessments with families and their dogs, is this: Believing that dogs are different with a culture and language all their own is difficult for most dog owners. They want their dogs to be a part of the family, and quickly act like human members. Most people are mortified when they have heard a growl coming from "my little Molly" the first time. Parents are more horrified when a child comes running in from the yard following a play session (without supervision or this wouldn't have happened) with a nip on the arm, scratches on the legs, and a puppy sitting confused in the yard. There is a reason for this 10 times out of 10: It's often from a lack of supervision (see "Children and Dogs" in Chapter Thirteen). At that point, the reason doesn't matter anymore, but what happens in the future does. Relationships are developed through awareness, education, and taking accountability for what happens in these relationships. Without training and supervision, the payoff for puppies is that they get to *play like puppies with children*. Children squeal, scream, and jump. This will incite nipping, pawing, and growling (usually play-growling, which would be perfectly appropriate in a litter of pups).

It's a lot to absorb, but what we invite you to do as you read *Train Your Dog, Change Your Life* is to integrate a little bit of all of this into your relationships with your dog and others. Teach and protect both children and dogs from failure. A little bit of prevention goes a long way.

Chapter Three

Recognizing Canine Calming Signals

The following overview is the essence of Turid Rugaas's theory on calming signals. Turid says, "Dogs, being flock animals, have a language for communication with each other. Canine language in general consists of a large variety of signals using body, face, ears, tail, sounds, movement and expression. The dog's innate ability to signal is easily lost or reinforced through life's experience. If we study the signals dogs use with each other and use them ourselves, we increase our ability to communicate with our dogs. Most noteworthy of all, canine signals which are used to maintain a healthy social hierarchy and resolution of conflict within the flock. These are skills which, when carried over to our own interactions with dogs can be highly beneficial to our relationship. Dogs have the ability to calm themselves in the face of a shock (fearful or stressful situation) and to calm each other as well. As an example let's consider the manner in which dogs meet each other. Dogs, which are worried in a social situation, can communicate concepts such as: 'I know you are the boss around here and I won't make trouble.' Furthermore, the boss dog is very apt to want the worried dog to realize that no trouble is intended. 'Don't worry, I'm in charge around here and I mean you no harm.' Dogs that do not signal properly can cause problems."

THE FUNDAMENTALS OF COMMUNICATION

For a moment, let's take ourselves away from established ideas and labels concerning displays of subordination, displacement activities, rituals, and drives, and let's think about canine body language as Rugaas does.

Those of us who have the opportunity to observe a group of well-socialized dogs interacting freely may see the following 12 calming signals:

1. Moving Slowly. A dog intending to use signals upon seeing another dog in the distance will start to move slowly. This exaggerated slow motion is a calming signal and can be used early and effectively when meeting. Joggers, cars, children, and bicycles may approach quickly and appear as a threat. This is something we should all keep in mind around our dogs.

2. Moving in an Arc. During first meetings, dogs will rarely approach each other nose to nose. Only dogs that are very sure of the outcome of a situation will attempt to meet head-on. More frequently, dogs approach each other in curving lines and walk beyond each other's nose to sniff rear ends while standing side to side.

Most apprehensive dogs are more easily approached if not confronted head-on. When approached from the side, one can gain the dog's confidence more readily. Unfortunately, dogs are constantly put into situations where they must accept a head-on confrontation. It's wise to condition our dogs to accept this eventuality gracefully, and without undue stress.

3. Sniffing the Ground. Dogs use their noses to explore their environment, but at times sniffing seems to have a different significance. Owners have attributed "out-of-context" sniffing to lack of concentration or stalling. Some say it's a displacement activity, i.e., "I don't know what to do ... so I'll sniff." Turid categorizes sniffing during times of stress as a "calming signal."

4. Sitting, Lying. These positions are probably the most graphic calming signals of all. You can see them being used in active play sessions. A dog will spontaneously drop when things get out of control.

How many dogs, when receiving a reprimand from the owner, will sit or lie down? Rugaas sees this as a signal that the dog is anxious and is trying to calm the owner down.

Lying down on their backs is a sign of submission. A familiar dog may show you this posture to get a belly rub. He is saying, "Hey, relax and give me a massage." At other times, this is a strong calming signal. Belly to the ground is a "mature" way for a confident dog to say to puppies and other dogs that they may be playing too hard. It's time to "settle-down." It's being a role model for puppies. Time to "chill-out." If your dog is bugging you, lie on the couch. If a dog is frightened of you, lie down on the floor. Get down to their level, by their side ... not in a confrontational posture. This will calm the dog down.

Sniffing during stressful situations is a calming signal.
(Illustration by Allison Smith)

5. Lip Licking. Every quick flicking of the tongue (licking nose) is a sign of pausing to reflect what might happen next. The dog is saying, "I'm not sure, so give me a second." It's another way for a dog to convey the same message, "Calm down." You will notice dogs licking when other dogs approach. Excessive licking, however, is a sign of stress or a health problem. Check with your veterinarian.

Licking is another calming signal. (Illustration by Allison Smith)

6. Turning Away (Blinking, Averting Eyes). When a dog approaches another, it's a very interesting moment in time for those individuals. Why then, do we see dogs looking away, exaggerating an eye blink, or turning their heads away from approaching dogs? Is it disinterest, distraction, or a calming signal?

People who work with dogs realize early in their careers that they can gain the confidence of a worried dog more quickly either by avoiding direct eye contact or by turning away with their backs or sides to the dog.

You can use turning when your dog shows signs of stress. If she or he jumps, turn away. A back presentation to the dog will create a moment of, "Huh? What's going on?" When your dog is acting out, taking away the reward, in this case your presence, will calm the behavior. Turn and walk away. Turning and/or walking away will let them know that this behavior is unacceptable. The key to shaping behavior is to watch for the behavior you want, then bring them back the reward: you and play.

Dogs can gain the trust of another dog by avoiding direct eye contact.
(Illustration by Allison Smith)

7. Yawning. Perhaps the most interesting of all the signals is yawning. It's one of our favorites because it's so easy to use and is effective. Yawning is a calming gesture to chill-out. It's a message that infers "take it easy." Dogs may yawn for no specific reason. You will recognize the difference by the situation you are in. For example, when a new dog team enters our training classroom, some dogs will bark, while others will yawn to calm the new pup and everyone else down. You can yawn to calm your dog if the surrounding environment is too exciting or tense.

Dogs will yawn to calm down other dogs; you can do the same to calm down your dog. (Illustration by Allison Smith)

8. Freezing. Ever hear the word *freeze-frame*? That is what freezing is with dogs. Your dog will stop, and remain absolutely still, when a larger dog comes too close or too fast and starts checking him out with its nose. A sniffing ritual ensues. The amount of communication occurring is vast and, in our opinion, a decision-making opportunity is created. Will this greeting be friendly? Do I know you? Was it pleasant?

You can use freezing to halt your dog in a precarious situation (dog gets loose accidentally and heads for the street). "Freeze" yourself and it can slow him down.

Two dogs engage in a sniffing ritual to check each other out.
(Illustration by Allison Smith)

9. Slow Movements. Slow movements have a very calming effect. Slowing movements (moving into freezing) also have the same effect. Your dog may use it with you or when he sees another dog. If you call your dog with an edge to your voice (irritation or command), you may see him start to slow down his movements. He is trying to calm you down. When there are a lot of things happening around the dog, he sloooows his movement to calm things down. Movements that fade to slow to hardly any movement have a very calming effect. When leashing up a frightened or easily excitable dog, move slowly.

10. Playbow. Your dog may try a playbow when he wants to become friends with another dog who isn't really quite sure about him. You can use this with a nervous dog, by imitating a playbow, as mentioned in "Dog Emotions" in Chapter Two, by crouching down and stretching your arms down and to the sides. You might just get one in return.

Dogs often use a playbow to ease tension when meeting unfamiliar dogs.
(Illustration by Allison Smith)

11. Wagging. People assume that a wagging tail means a "happy" dog. Regrettably, this is not always the case. Wags have many more meaningful signals, just as human smiles can run the gamut from sly, cocky, to sincerely joyful. The next time you see a dog wagging her tail, stand back and look at the whole picture. The position of the tail and the particular situation needs careful assessment before deciding. If a dog is crawling and whining as she comes to greet you with the tail lowered and wagging slowly, then this is a white flag. The dog is trying to calm you down ("Don't kill me"), probably due to a previous association. Wagging is difficult for humans to use with dogs. Laughing is the human version of tail wagging.

12. Splitting. Splitting is when your dog physically goes between two other dogs and/or humans. A dog may stand between two other critters when a physical situation becomes tense. When your dogs get tense (if you have more than one), you can "split" them by standing in-between. Kady, our Newfie, used to stand between puppies and adult dogs if she sensed that the puppies were frightened or uneasy. Kady would stand between us if we were arguing. She would yawn, lick her nose, and then give us a look as if to imply, "Please, take a deep breath; nothing can be that bad and you're upsetting me." Then, she would let out a sigh, walk away, and lie down as if to say, "Silly humans, what's the big deal?" Like most dogs, she was a good barometer of our behavior.

DOES SIGNALING WORK FOR ALL DOGS?

As with some humans, some dogs do not play by the rules. There are many reasons a dog might lose the inborn ability to use calming signals properly. Puppies learn valuable lessons from their environment. One must be very careful about the company a puppy keeps or the pup might learn that calming signals are of no use.

If a pup, while displaying calming signals, encounters a dog lacking respect for appropriate body language and is attacked, much ground has been lost. This pup might learn to use threatening actions as a life insurance policy instead of calming signals. Luckily, with most dogs, it takes more than one or two unfortunate incidents to extinguish signaling. Calming is a very dominant instinct in dogs. However, it's a good idea to protect young dogs from interacting with unnatural, angry dogs. Safe, friendly dogs with good signals are the best teachers a young dog can have. Puppy classes are helpful in teaching these lessons, but can do more harm than good if inappropriate dogs are allowed to interact.

Some owners hamper a dog's attempt to communicate with other dogs or humans by inhibiting them with leashes. Yes, by all means, dogs should be on leash. No, it's not safe to turn your dog loose to communicate freely with an unknown dog. But be aware that you could be helping your dog get into trouble by preventing appropriate body language. A more prudent plan is for you and your pet to keep your distance from an unknown entity.

Whether on purpose or unintentionally, some dogs have been taught to ignore signals. Many responsible owners seek dog-educational classes as an opportunity to train their dogs. Here's a typical class exercise: Owners command their dogs to sit-stay. Dogs happily comply. The class instructor now asks owners and dogs to take turns weaving among the sitting dogs. This is fine in an advanced class of dogs with well-known temperaments. In a beginner's class, a handler might be asked by an instructor to prevent a fearful dog from signaling, which would send a distinct message to other dogs "calm down, I'm nervous." This dog may hesitate, lick, sniff, or arc. If the owner/handler pulls on the leash, then this could result in the dog's hesitating to use his God-given instinct to signal in the future, thus preventing the defusing of a potentially hostile situation. A little bit of positive coaxing is okay, but forcing an uncertain dog into an uncertain situation is not.

PRACTICAL APPLICATIONS OF SIGNALING

We have the opportunity to observe many scenarios with families and dogs at Dog Talk training classes. It never ceases to amaze us how resilient and adaptive most puppies and adult dogs are regardless of their past experiences. Some pups will linger behind owners and under chairs. Nervous older dogs from shelters will sit with their eyeballs popping out of their heads because of the numerous transitions they have had to undergo.

You can use calming signals (like yawning) to ease your dog through stressful situations, such as encountering jackhammer noises during a walk.
(Illustration by Allison Smith)

We encourage you to let you and your pups be yourselves. Take a while to adjust. In the meantime, observe the pups and look for signals. Are they attempting to come "out from behind the chair"? Is a paw sticking out? Then, praise them. Usually by week three, puppies will join in. Older dogs will discover that it is safe and they will become more confident too.

"To be able to communicate, to be actually understood by dogs, that is a wonderful feeling for people and dogs alike. Calming signals are the key and seeing through that opened door has been looking into a childhood dream of talking to the animals.

"In many cases, dogs become hysterical when I answer them in their language. It is like someone long lost in the jungle and suddenly at the edge of despair hears his native tongue being spoken. Maybe that is why rehabilitated dogs remember me years after they have been here." —Turid Rugaas

Chapter Four

Getting the Desired Results from Your Dog

To get the results that you want from your dog, you need to "shape" their behaviors. That means if you reward desired behaviors, they will increase in probability and with greater frequency.

Whether training dogs or teaching people, it's all one and the same when it comes to behavior shaping, modifying a behavior, and learning from a consequence of a behavior. The major difference between people and other species, for the purpose of both this book and dog training, is how we reason. Humans have a more sophisticated (and sometimes more complicated) way of dealing with situations. We plan, premeditate, and have a conscience. Our emotions can range from joyful to miserable, angry to happy, fearful to confident; we feel guilty and live in denial all in the course of a day. Dogs, on the other hand, are clever creatures who awaken in a state of spontaneity. They decide instantly what to do based on previous results. They choose a behavior for survival needs (eat, drink, eliminate), work (herding, retrieving, hunting, rescuing, companionship), and activities that relieve boredom (play, entertainment). Most dogs are naturally curious. Based on what happened previously, if anything, the dog will proceed to either do it again, or not, depending on the consequence.

Every creature, then, has a repertoire of behavior that she has performed at least once. If any of these behaviors are reinforced, they will start to increase in probability and with greater frequency. "Down" is a behavior that occurs at the operant level in dogs. Dogs lie down naturally (sleep, rest, and roll over). Simply rewarding instances of down will increase the probability of getting a down posture from your dog with a request.

There are some behaviors that dogs will not offer spontaneously. These behaviors are described as not occurring "at the operant level." There aren't any responses to reinforce so it becomes necessary to shape the behavior. For example: Luring (using food) and rewarding instances of down in appropriate places, like lying down on, or approaching, the mat in the family room, is shaping a particular behavior (where to lie down, when, and for how long). Good shaping is a smooth series of segues between continuous reinforcement as a new level is being achieved and variable reinforcement as that achievement solidifies and the occasional even better response can be reinforced selectively. That was a mouthful. Don't panic. Take a deep breath. There's more on reinforcement later.

This is not profound or complex information. It has been written about and bantered around for decades. To simplify things, let's just say dogs do what they do because it works for them. Isn't that an easy concept to comprehend? Like humans, they do something, get results, and based on the results (or consequences), will do it again or not. If this sounds rather nebulous, you are absolutely on the mark—it is. This leaves a wide-open space for behaviors to occur for a number of different reasons. Undoubtedly, you will not desire your dog to display many of these behaviors. Therefore, the concept of behavior shaping in its simplest format is to learn how to shape the behaviors of choice. This can apply to you or your dog.

Let's explore behavioral shaping further by breaking this down into the basics of what you need to understand about how it works. If this excites you, there are several suggested readings at the back of the book.

HOW BEHAVIORS ARE SHAPED

This summary of the history of behavior shaping and dog training will help you to focus on a wider perspective of how behaviors are shaped. Keep in mind that behaviors are not always shaped by the most obvious things or events.

Watson's Little Albert

J. B. Watson (1878–1958), a psychologist who worked at Johns Hopkins University and the University of Chicago, is known as the father of a movement called behaviorism. When we share the following story in training class, inevitably someone will grimace and say, "How awful!," so we always preface it by saying, "There's a happy ending."

In the case of little Albert, Watson emphasized the need to get away from concentrating on thoughts and feelings and move toward the scientific, experimental study of behavior. Albert was an 11-month-old boy who was allowed to play freely with a white rat. A loud noise was presented whenever Albert reached out and touched the rat. The noise was loud enough to startle Albert. In one week, whenever the rat was presented Albert would cry, even without the noise. Aha! He also generalized his fear to other things, including a white dog, a white rabbit, and a white Santa Claus mask. If this experiment had continued, chances are Albert would have cried at anything white. Obviously, it did not, and Watson did modify Albert's behavior by changing the association and desensitizing. How? Simply by presenting something positive to Albert in the presence of that same white rat.

How can this help you with your puppy? It can help you understand what has happened when you are dealing with fear of any sort. External criteria are shaping behaviors with our dogs all the time.

Pavlov's Bell

The name Ivan Pavlov (1849–1936) should ring a bell. The Russian physiologist studied digestion in dogs and observed that his subjects would salivate before food was placed in their mouths. He thought the dogs were associating the lab assistants or the sound of the door opening with the food. He tested this theory by ringing a bell just before feeding time. After a number of trials, ringing the bell caused the dogs to salivate. Pavlov's work in classical, or respondent, conditioning explains reflexive behavior like salivation.

Classical conditioning is the pairing of something that has no meaning with something that has intrinsic meaning, so that they become associated. Let's make this simple with an example: Food has intrinsic meaning to dogs because they will die without nutrition. On their own, cookie jars have no meaning. Dogs quickly learn to associate the sight and sound of the cookie jar with cookies because the sight and sound of the cookie jar reliably predicts cookies. This same phenomenon explains why dogs get excited when you put your coat on and grab your car keys or take the leash out. It's what the picture has come to mean through repeated associations with things of intrinsic value to the dog. Our dogs have mastered every nuance of our body language to the point where a movement in our chairs will trigger a response of a look and alert eyes. The dogs always seem to know if it will lead to biscuits, outside, a walk, a good sniff, or time for bed.

Skinner, The Disney Dog, and Real Life

When a puppy or dog joins a human family, it's kind of like entering a giant Skinner's input-output box. B. F. Skinner (1904–1990) was influenced by Watson and Pavlov. As a doctoral student at Harvard University, Skinner discovered that he could systematically change the behavior of rats by giving the rats a food reward for pressing a lever.

Although Edward Thorndike is often credited with being the first to outline operant conditioning concepts, Skinner was the first to widely publicize the new theory. Operant conditioning is the conditioning of operants, a category of behaviors like sitting, grabbing laundry, or biting someone. Operants get stronger through conditioning in the same way that muscles get stronger through physical workouts. If when the dog sits she receives a healthy treat, the operant "sitting" gets reinforced and becomes more probable. If a dog nips a child, and the child squeaks, what happens? It depends on the dog and the consequence of biting the child. If an adult is not present, and the dog has not learned that biting humans hurts, the dog may respond with excitement and bite again. All dogs are predatory by nature, some stronger than others. There is no magic wand here. Training and the environment change probabilities.

♦ ♦ ♦

Thorndike's Law of Effect says responses that produce rewards tend to increase in frequency.

♦ ♦ ♦

As Jean Donaldson articulates in her book *The Culture Clash*, the Disney dog is Lassie, and Lassie can do no wrong. Lassie is very intelligent, solves complex problems, understands values, has morals, and is a surrogate child, babysitter, husband, and therapist. On the other hand, Skinner's dog depicts the input-output box. Let's apply this to real life. For example, a dog is reprimanded every time he chews the furniture. The owner reprimands the dog, usually after the dog has enjoyed the pure entertainment of chewing. Now, the dog refrains from chewing in front of the owner. The owner's (Disney) view would be: My dog learns from the reprimand that chewing is wrong. My dog resents being left alone and to get back at me, he chews. When the owner gets home, the dog "feels" guilty.

Skinner's view, which is more accurate, is: The dog learns that chewing furniture is dangerous when the owner is present, and safe when the owner is gone. The dog becomes slightly anxious when left alone and feels better when he chews. When the owner arrives home, the dog will act submissive, anxious, or fearful in an attempt to avoid punishment. The dog knows he will be punished because it has happened before. He associates it with the owner's homecoming. What he doesn't know is why. There is no connection unless the connection is made instantly. Timing is a crucial factor that we will explore more of as we continue on.

Here's an easy equation for those of you who like equations: $A + B = C$. That is: Antecedent (events that occur before a behavior) + Behavior = Consequence. If you remember this, you'll always know that something happens (a precursor), then a behavior occurs, followed by a consequence for that behavior. This in turn prompts a dog (or human) to choose the next behavior.

In human settings, there are many examples of stimuli that control and shape our choices of behavior. When we are driving down the road and see a red traffic light (an antecedent), we brake to stop the car. Braking is the behavior. The consequence, in this case, is a good one because we do not get broadsided or ticketed.

CONCEPTS AND EXAMPLES OF BEHAVIOR SHAPING

As the preceding examples demonstrate, behavior shaping using positive reinforcement is an excellent way to get the desired results from your dog. Truthfully, for most dogs, the prime goal is to please their owners and do so without unpleasant altercations. As we continue our journey through *Train Your Dog, Change Your Life*, you will learn more about behavior shaping and how to use it to your advantage in every aspect of your life.

The following definitions and examples will help to clarify what behavior shaping using different reinforcement theories is about.

Reinforcement Theory

Whatever the training task—whether keeping a toddler quiet in public, training a dog, or coaching a team—it will go faster and better and be more fun if you know how to use positive reinforcement. The basic laws of reinforcement are simple, but applying them is more of a challenge. It requires quick thinking, timing, coordination, and an ability to play games. This may sound simple, but many folks prefer hard work to games. Reinforcements are relative, not absolute. Rain is a positive reinforcement for ducks, a negative one for most cats, and a matter of indifference to cows.

Positive Reinforcement

Positive reinforcement is the training of choice for us, especially for puppies. Most trainers, however, employ a variety of techniques to achieve results, depending on particular circumstances. With positive reinforcement, the opportunities for pleasant and effective behavior shaping and training are boundless. The opportunities are exciting because with positive reinforcement you can increase the quality of a current behavior and endlessly teach new ones.

Positive reinforcement is anything that, when occurring in conjunction with an act, tends to increase the probability that the act will occur again. It's something the dog wants: food, pats, hugs, praise, playing games. Food is not positive reinforcement if you're full. To be reinforcing, the item chosen needs to be something that the subject (dog or human) really desires. *You* can be the positive reinforcement or life reward. If your dog loves being with you, then giving him attention is positive reinforcement. This can get tricky, so be careful. You can diminish the value of any reward or positive reinforcer by overusing it.

Negative Reinforcement

Negative reinforcement is utilized more often then we would like to admit. The word has a "negative" connotation, but in reality, it's quite effective if used fairly and appropriately. Succinctly, the moment that anyone puts a collar and leash on a dog and tugs the first time the dog lunges forward (which most dogs will do), and the dog stops, then this is negative reinforcement. If you are a super trainer and smile the very instant the dog looked back at you when you did the tugging, then your smile was saying, "What a good dog." This can be an excellent learning experience. Realistically, how many people can do this or have the time for it? You want your dog to associate the collar, leash, and being with you as something positive, not an active game of tug and pull.

+ + +

"Between Stimulus and Response, there is a space. In that space lies our freedom and power to choose our response. In our response lies our growth and our freedom." —Stephen R. Covey, The Seven Habits of Highly Effective People

+ + +

Negative reinforcement is anything that, occurring in conjunction with an act, tends to increase or decrease the probability the act will occur again. Did that tug on the leash increase or decrease your dog pulling? You need to assess this carefully. This is something that a dog will work at to avoid, and it can range from mild to severe. Negative reinforcement is not punishment. A dog cannot avoid punishment; it comes after the behavior. One can't avoid punishment by changing one's mind or an action, the behavior has already occurred. Negative reinforcement can be avoided by changing the behavior, pronto. For example, your dog is about to hop onto the forbidden zone (the sofa). By some miracle, he looks and notices you standing behind him, glaring. He changes his mind, due to past association, and lies on the floor instead.

Negative reinforcement can be an appropriate method of shaping behavior provided it's contingent upon the behavior and that you cease glaring when the dog decides "better lie on the floor," the correct response. The same holds true for tugging on the leash. The moment the dog eases up on the leash, you must smile. The key is to stop giving the negative reinforcement when the dog's behavior improves even slightly. Ensure the dog sees it as a consequence of his own act, not something that you do arbitrarily and all the time. Behaviors learned via negative reinforcement usually stay where they are. They don't get better or worse. This is the major difference between negative reinforcement and positive reinforcement. Positive reinforcement has boundless limits because a dog, or a person, will want to perform behavior that they know will get rewarded.

Punishment

While writing this book, we kept going back and forth on whether or not to even talk about punishment. We decided to summarize it briefly, because punishment has been too deeply woven into society to disappear effortlessly. We're raised with punishment and saturated with examples of it throughout our lifetime, so it becomes acceptable. Examples of punishment in dog training are: severe verbal reprimands, swatting, spanking, hitting, spraying lemon juice into the face, shaking by the scruff of the neck, leash jerking or hanging, and, of course, abuse of high-tech electrical equipment. These are common interventions that have been used too frequently, after the unacceptable behavior has occurred, and sometimes by inexperienced people.

Punishment causes displeasure for both the owner and the dog, and, most importantly, it does not eradicate a behavior. Punishment merely stuns behavior. It interrupts and buys you a temporary suppression of the behavior. That's it. When you use punishment, you may bomb the dog's whole repertoire of good behavior as well, not to mention squashing his or her spirit.

Dogs are obedient to the laws of learning and association, not to us. Punishment ceases a behavior but does not teach a behavior. Ask yourself, "What can the dog do with the kids?" How about "sit," pronto? Teach it. Then, teach "up" and "off," but always request a "sit" first. We haven't met a dog yet who can jump, chew, knock grandma over, and indiscriminately eliminate or lick himself in front of company when he is sitting.

If you plan on using punishment, think twice. You must have a second-nature sense of these conditions to use punishment effectively: Punishment must be immediate, big, and doled out every time the dog misbehaves, or it's useless. Always associate it *only to that behavior*. Teaching what it is you do expect must always follow punishment. Otherwise, it's cruel and abusive treatment. Positive reinforcement training is much easier; you'll feel better about yourself and the results last longer.

Reinforcement Schedules

Rewarding behavior over and over increases the tendency of that behavior. For example, "down" becomes a target behavior when a dog is reinforced each and every time he lies down. The behavior will eventually plateau out in frequency; stop rewarding the behavior each and every time it occurs. You will reward most of the time, then half of the time, then sometimes, then occasionally. The reason for this is to facilitate the shaping process and make the behavior more resilient to extinction.

If your dog is used to getting rewarded every time and then suddenly isn't, the behavior goes into extinction; it stops happening because the treats stop coming. Consider the difference between a soft drink machine and a slot machine. You expect a soft drink every time you put money into the soda machine. If the machine does not produce a soda more than a couple of times, you try another strategy: body slamming the machine or calling an authority for help and reimbursement. With a slot machine, the rules are different. You don't expect to get rewarded every time. So, you keep putting money in the machine in hopes of the winning combination. You await the jackpot.

Jackpot!

Reward the behavior that knocks your socks off. You are absolutely thrilled and excited that your dog came over to you with his leash in his mouth, sat, and looked in anticipation of a walk. This is the best response you have received. This reward constitutes many treats, praise, a game of retrieve or hide-and-seek. Savor the moment and reward the behavior you really, really desire.

Fixed Interval

A fixed-interval reinforcement schedule would be rewarding the dog every five or ten seconds if he is still doing the behavior at the time. This is effective for incrementally reinforcing behaviors and increasing attention span, like having your dog watch you (or down-stay) for five seconds, then reinforce with treat; 10 seconds, reinforce with treat; one minute, reinforce; and so on. (For 30-minute down-stays, see "Down-Stay" in Chapter Ten.)

Variable Interval

Once a behavior is learned, you must start reinforcing it occasionally rather than constantly to maintain it at the present level. This law is the crux of the behavior-shaping process. Variable-interval schedules are good for installing duration into such behavior as stays, heels, and getting attention. Variable intervals increase enthusiasm and help to ferret out boredom for both trainer and dog. The dog realizes the treat (or a game of retrieve) is coming, but isn't sure when. It becomes a game of when, where, what do I do, and how long will it take to get this.

Differential Schedules

Trainers most often use differential schedules. As soon as a behavior is put on schedule, the trainer/owner selects the best example of the behavior for reinforcement. Many behaviors are not all or nothing–type behaviors. Select the one you like the best—cuter, faster, straighter, better than before—and reward it. This will crank up the quality of performance from your dog. How stringent the criteria or behavior you are looking for depends entirely on you, your efforts, and timing. Timing is an absolute necessity in training or shaping behaviors.

The results you receive from your dog will relate to your efforts in explaining your expectations to them in a way that he can understand. It's about behavior-shaping savvy. If you really want to get your dog to respond to your request, you have to make it meaningful, not blase. Dogs are keenly aware of cajoling and meaningless gestures.

Stimulus Control

Anything that causes some kind of behavioral response is a stimulus. Some stimuli can cause responses without learning or training: We blink at bright lights, jump at loud noises, and hold our noses at offensive smells. Other stimuli are learned through associations. They become recognizable signals for behavior: Traffic lights make us stop and go, we leap to answer phones, and we close our eyes when a squirrel gets run over. These are called conditioned, or secondary, stimuli.

Conditioned Reinforcers/Reward Markers

A cue or signal will tell the dog that positive reinforcement has just been won, rather than willy-nilly doling out of treats, toys, or game playing. The timing needs to be precise and sometimes we want to signal the dog at a distance. The signal is called a conditioned reinforcer or bridging stimulus. The conditioned reinforcer becomes associated with the real (unconditioned) reinforcer by repeated pairing. It's called a bridging stimulus because it bridges the time gap between the behavior you liked and the actual reinforcement. It's kind of like a performance review with a salary increase. You wait six months, then get a good review and a raise for a job well done. The difference for dogs is that the reward needs to be immediate, e.g., a liver treat. They cannot comprehend a six-month wait. The liver treat is the unconditioned reinforcer.

Unconditioned Reinforcers

The dog doesn't learn to like and work for food. It comes with the package. She learns to like and work for the praise, play, or click that has come to mean food. It's an association of what is to come that leaves a dog wiggly with anticipation.

Systematic Desensitization

Systematic desensitization is the same technique used by counselors for people with phobias who are excessively afraid of spiders, dogs, or flying in airplanes. The person is taught to relax and then is introduced to the fearful stimulus at whatever level he or she can tolerate (without anxiety) while practicing a relaxation exercise. Then the stimulus is gradually intensified at whatever rate the subject can handle, always building on success.

The real-life necessity of having to leave dogs alone requires that owners slowly build on desensitizing a dog who is phobic or experiencing separation anxiety (an over-diagnosed disorder, in our opinion). The idea is to build tolerance slowly, not to flood the dog with long periods of being alone. Begin with small home-alone sessions with the dog confined in an area where no damage can be done. Then increase the time left alone.

Using a safety cue, such as a radio, helps during training sessions. The radio becomes a signal to the dog that only short, nonanxiety-producing absences are in store. It's not the radio per se that relaxes the dog, but rather the reliable pairing with tolerable levels of solitude that establish it as relaxing. Homecomings should be pleasant and nonanxiety-producing (not too much emotion). This time can begin with minutes and increased to several hours. Begin slowly. Quicker or more is not always better.

THE TEN LAWS OF SHAPING BEHAVIORS

Now that you have an overview of the basic concepts, you're probably asking, "How does all this stuff apply to me?" Here are ten rules to keep in mind as you try to shape your dog's behavior:

1. Raise criteria in increments small enough so that your dog always has a realistic chance for reinforcement.

2. Train one behavior at a time; don't try to shape for two behaviors simultaneously.

3. Always put the current level of response onto a variable-interval reinforcement schedule before adding or raising criteria.

4. When introducing a new behavior, temporarily relax the old ones.

5. Stay ahead of your dog. Plan your shaping program completely so that if he makes sudden progress you're aware of what to reinforce next.

6. Don't change shapers in midstream; you can have several trainers per trainee but stick to one shaper per behavior.

7. If one shaping procedure is not eliciting progress, find another; there are as many ways to get behavior as there are trainers to think them up.

8. Don't interrupt a training session gratuitously—that constitutes a punishment and/or a lack of desire on your part that you really want your dog to respond. If you treat a training session as a low priority, the dog will, too.

9. If behavior deteriorates, "go back to kindergarten"—quickly review the whole shaping process with a series of easy reinforcements.

10. End each session on a high note. Snapshot small successes. Don't bag the whole process because of one mistake; learn from it. Quit while you're ahead. If you feel as though you are decomposing on the spot, hit your "pause" button, take a deep breath, go for a walk, and de-stress. Ask yourself, "Will this be important a week, six months, or a year from now?"

"A bend in the road is not the end of the road, if you remember to take the turn." —Joan Lunden

✦ ✦ ✦

By shaping your dog's behaviors and learning different approaches to dog training, you can achieve a trusting relationship with your canine companion.

A TRUSTING RELATIONSHIP

Who wants to be obedient? Not us! These days, most couples, depending on the culture, take the "obey" part of the vows out when they marry.

Webster's New World College Dictionary defines obedient as "obeying or willing to obey; submissive."

Who wants to be obedient anyway? Behavior shaping using positive reinforcement is an excellent way to get the desired results with your dog, while building a relationship built on trust. (Photo by Gary Ross)

Historically, the connotation and meaning of dog-obedience training comes from the world wars. It's a military style of training that still exists today in many training courses.

Can you think of a more submissive and compliant creature than a puppy? In most cases, she is willing and able to do practically anything we ask (within reason) just for the yuck of it. Therefore, the word *obedience* seems, to us anyway, understood. It isn't something we need to focus on or print a dozen times on training brochures, handouts, or in this book.

In that sense, we have a strenuous time calling any behavior shaping or relationship building with a dog "obedience" training. During assessments with potential students, we refer to it over and over again as teaching, and they respond, "But I want an obedient dog." Our typical reply is to ask, "Okay then, tell me how you would like to achieve that?" or "What are your goals for you and your dog?" That usually is enough to prompt them to consider what they are really looking for, and that is a well-trained, reliable, fairly predictable, healthy, confident, trusting, and joyful dog for themselves and their children, not merely an obedient dog.

For example: We respect police officers in most circumstances, right? However, if they pulled you over for no particular reason, flashed a badge in your face, told you to get out of the car, then zapped you with a stun gun because you wouldn't comply, what would your reaction be?

Using this metaphor within the realm of family dog training, we perceive obedience to be of little use. The trainer/owner would be holding prong collars, remote controls for the electronic bark collar, cattle prods, lemon-juice sprayer, jerking leashes, and shouting demands.

The dog does need a pack leader. We all need some guidance, boundaries, values, and a sense of right and wrong to survive in our environments. Dogs need to perceive someone as the leader to make their jobs and lives easier. They need this even more for survival in a human world. That leader provides boundaries, guidance, and education.

THE THREE SHALLS OF DOG TRAINING

People ask us all the time, "If there were only three things that you could do to train your dog, what would they be?" We are really happy to answer this question, because there are three things, which, if done consistently with your dog, will enrich your relationship with awareness, education, mutual understanding, and trust. We call them "The Three Shalls."

These Shalls are easy to do and have a profound impact on your relationship with your dog. We perceive them as behavior modification for both parties (human and dog). The Three Shalls are:

1. You shall reward the behaviors you want.

2. You shall implement a "You do something for me, I'll do something for you" program.

3. And, you shall *never* reprimand your dog after calling him to you.

Sound easy? Yes, they are. Are they effective? Absolutely!

Shall #1: You shall reward the behaviors you want

Let's face it, how many of our dogs think at least one of their names is, "No! No! Bad dog!"? More than a few, we bet. It's very easy to fall into the trap of following the dog around, correcting as we go along, and attaching her name to the correction. A gem of advice: Unless you live in a multiple-dog household and need to spot out specifically which dog you are reprimanding, do not use your dog's name when you are angry or giving corrections. Your dog is clever. She will quickly figure out from the tone of your voice and body language that something is amiss. If she associates her name to your voice, it will be detrimental when you call her in the future for pleasure.

Eventually, the dog builds itself a catalog of don'ts for each situation. It's far more effective to say, "Yes! Yes! Good dog!" for those things they do that we really want and like. Help them build a catalog of desired behaviors. Ensure that the "do" catalog is much larger than the "don't" one. Remember: Praise the behavior you want when you get it.

What Governs How We Behave?

Think about how we react in any given situation. Presented with a set of circumstances, we guess based on what we have learned in the past. For example, when we sit in a new car and want to turn on the headlights, we have to look around for the right control or use the manual. When we find the right page in the manual and subsequently the right switch, *voilá*, the lights come on. Reward. Sure, but during the process we may have also washed both the front and back windows, attempted to program our preferred radio stations, played around with the AC and heat controls, and blown the horn. Who cares? The point is we made an attempt at accomplishing a task and learned something else along the way as a perk.

Applying this concept to our dogs, when they are presented with a situation, like us, they guess at the "right" answer based upon their experiences. The major difference is that they do not have the benefit of relying on a manual. They need us to point them to the right control and/or praise them when they find it themselves. If we were to only use corrections for our dogs, then, for each situation, they would have to sift through their impressions of don'ts in the catalog (for that particular situation) to see what does and doesn't apply. Wouldn't it be much simpler to praise the suitable behavior in the first place? Wouldn't this increase the odds of them getting it right? Of course it would. The sifting process disappears. The catalog pops out the right answer the first time. We go right to the headlight switch. It becomes habit and a way to get what we want; turn the headlights on with ease so we can see the light!

As you can see, this works equally well with dogs and humans. Creating a catalog in our heads of positive self-talk tapes rather than negative self-talk increases our self-esteem and a desire to do more. We all relish "attaboys" and "attagirls" as universal scratches on our tummies. They need to be employed as often as possible. Every morning, awaken with the notion of gratefulness. Even if you had a bad evening, and this might be difficult, create the illusion that today will be a new beginning. You are alive and share a life with a dog. That in and of itself is a blessing.

Does this mean that we stop saying no? No. In addition to praise for getting the behavior that you want, we use something that trainers call instructive reprimands (IR). An instructive reprimand is just letting the dog know what they're doing wrong rather than just saying "no," which can wear out extremely fast. For example, say our little puppy has an accident in the house and *we catch him in the act*. Rather than just scolding him ("No! No! Bad dog!"), we pick him up and whisk him outside (if that's where he is supposed to go) while saying "Outside!" (IR). Then when he finishes outside, praise him profusely ("Yes! Yes! Good dog!"). By doing this we are reducing the pages in his catalog for eliminating. We are minimizing the excessive "babbling" that dogs really don't need anyway. He is far less likely to make a mistake next time and it will be less confusing, as he will know that "outside" means "outside." He won't have to siphon through the emotional repertoire of, "Oh no, not again, not in the house, my beautiful carpet, you bad dog. ... You are supposed to go outside, whose job was it anyway to watch you today? ... Blah, blah, blah." You get the picture.

Shall #2: You shall implement a "You do something for me, I'll do something for you" program

First ask the dog to do something for you and then let the life reward become the positive reinforcer. No free lunch here. Our dogs rely on us for almost everything they need to live: food, shelter, and companionship. We are the centers of their universes. However, most of us misunderstand and very often disrespect these values. Our dogs get a lot of this stuff for free. Generally, we, as people, have to work for our rewards—a paycheck, recognition by our peers, and so forth. Why not have the dog work for the things they want? It will give them someplace to expend puppy energy in a positive way, and it will be mentally stimulating. Make them "sit-down-and-stay" before they get their meal. Have them sit before petting. "Oh, you want a scratch, lie down and roll over ..." This principle can be extended to the stuff we call "life rewards." A life reward is something that the dog wants anyway; for example, going outside for a walk or a ride in the car. "Sit-stay-wait" until you open the back door for him to run (assuming you have a confined, safe area for him to run in). Think of how powerful a tool this can become. Now instead of having only two or three more formal training sessions during the day, we have those plus 20 or 30 quick, informal sessions as well. No free lunch here. Plus, contemplate on what this does for your dog. It gives him a purpose and a job to do. All dogs need this desperately, even if it is something as simple as "go find the biscuit." They enjoy doing what pleases us. They enjoy it even more if it includes something that they excel at because they're dogs.

Shall #3: You shall *never* reprimand your dog after calling him to you

How often has this happened to you? Your dog sees something he likes (for that moment) more than he likes you. He leaves to investigate. You follow in hot pursuit. During the pursuit, you visualize doing unmentionables to your dog. You call his name, he runs faster. Then, in a moment of triumph, light dawns, he turns and eagerly sprints towards you. What do you do? Do you imagine the two of you coming together in an embrace? Or, do you visualize wringing his bloody neck? The right answer, at least metaphorically, is the embrace. You have to praise him. Why? Because he came to you when you called him. It's essential that when your dog comes to you, that action is *always* pleasurable.

The way to ensure that dogs come when we call them is to make ourselves more interesting to them than the environment. They should never, ever be afraid of their human companion. Respect us, yes, but fearful of us, no. That's a tall order. The first step down that road is to teach them that only good (and hopefully great) things happen when they come to you. Remember, if you have to reprimand your companion, always go to them first, and always make it an instructive reprimand. Teach the behavior you're looking for. Anything else is simply punishment. Be your dog's friend!

Keep these Three Shalls in mind as you shape the behaviors that you want.

Section Two

Relationship Training

In Section One, we explored the fundamentals of relationship training: Creating a safe place, understanding canine body language, recognizing canine calming signals, and getting the desired results from your dog. We invite you and your dog to join us now by integrating all the theory that you have learned into a more structured approach for developing your skills with your dog.

Chapter Five will introduce training exercises essential for puppies and new dogs in your household. Chapters Six through Eleven provide a step-by-step roadmap, showing you and your family how to teach your puppy or dog the basic skills to survive (and thrive) in today's hectic society. We will describe voice and hand signals, form, and footwork.

Training is an art form. In a sense, think of this as dancing with your dog. It needs to be individually developed into your own unique style and practiced on a regular basis. But, as things go, you can't tango without learning how to foxtrot first.

The program will allow you to begin slowly and progress at a rate that you choose. Remember, don't throttle ahead too quickly or you'll spin out. The puppy will get confused, children will get distraught and give up, and you will get a headache.

Regression is a virtue here. Don't be afraid to regress if something isn't working instantaneously. For example, you are in Week #3 of your lessons. You proudly believe that you have accomplished a good sit-down-and-stay for 20 seconds. The puppy always "does it at home." Now, it's time to venture to the park. You can't wait; you arrive ready to shine. What happens? Your puppy decides that her mouth is sore, she's cutting teeth this week, she needs to eliminate, and she wants to have a good sniff. The dog is interested in everything in the park except you. Bewilderment sets in. You hang your head in dismay. The other dog teams you've been meeting at the park seem to be doing so well. How do you handle this? There's no shame or blame needed here. Toss that away. Buck up and regress. It's no big deal. This simply isn't a good day for training, yet.

Drop back to an easier task. Take a deep breath and think. What can your puppy do successfully? Figure out what will motivate your puppy (a toy, food treat). You know better than anyone does. Smile and simplify the exercise. Snapshot the behaviors you want. Catch your puppy in the act of doing something right, praise and reward.

Are you ready? Let's continue on to what we guarantee will help create a better relationship between you and your dog (possibly even other humans). If you follow through for the next six weeks, honing your skills and teaching your puppy with these step-by-step, easy-to-follow exercises, you can only benefit. You absolutely will gain awareness and education.

Remember — attitude, an open mind, and a careful sense of humor are little things that make a big difference.

Chapter Five

Basic Training for Puppies

From the moment a new puppy (or adult dog) joins your household, you, your family, and friends should integrate the exercises in this chapter into her daily experiences. This should be a team effort. Otherwise, everything that you accomplish will be botched by the first person who doesn't do it.

It's natural for everyone to want to hug and pick up puppies. That's fine. Pups do not stay little for very long, particularly some of the giant breeds. However, you must be a leader here and establish a set of easy-to-follow guidelines for everyone. Anyone who comes in contact with the pup should ask for a "sit." Give people a healthy biscuit or piece of kibble to entice the pup into a sit before petting or playing. (See "Week #1," later in this chapter, for instructions.) Before we get into the training exercises, let's take a look at the basic training equipment that you'll need.

TOOLS OF THE TRAINING TRADE

To train effectively, you need the right tools. Unless you've spent the last 10 years on Venus, you can't help but notice the explosion in the pet-product business. There's always some new training "thingy" for pooch problems ranging from housetraining to pulling.

Let's review some of the basic tools that you'll want to use for training your dog. (Tools like the clicker, Kongs, and activity balls are described elsewhere in this book.)

Collars

There are many different kinds of collars available. The old standby is the buckle collar. These come in all colors, shapes and sizes, in nylon or leather, with metal or plastic hardware, and some with studs (to each his own). A basic collar is like your basic screwdriver and pliers — nice and safe, but they won't offer much control.

Another popular collar is the choke collar. These come in various shapes, sizes, and colors. Some are made from nylon, some from chain. They offer the sense of control, but they are ripe for abuse. The choke can be pulled as tight as the trainer wants, a potentially bad situation for the dogs. Plus, we always see someone who has the choke on backwards, or way too big to allow a fit over that Rottie or St. Bernard head. Therefore, it doesn't release properly when there is slack in the leash or it hangs down around the chest area, the strongest pulling areas on most dogs. The collar should always be worn with the ring coming under the dog's neck, depending on what side you walk them on. So if you walk your dog on the left (traditional) side, the collar should form a letter "P" when looking at the dog's head. The chokes are the handsaws in our tool chest. Useful, but we can slip and cut ourselves if we're not careful.

Metal prong collars can be very effective when used properly, but the metal prongs are an invitation for abuse. This is getting into the power tools of the training trade. Read and understand the directions. There is also the problem of perception. We know prong collars can be safe and humane, but that layperson over there doesn't. To her, the Pit Bull puppy with the prong collar must be vicious.

Our favorite collar is the Premier adjustable martingale collar. The collar has two loops, a large adjustable one for the head, and a smaller loop (connected to each other by two rings) to connect to the leash. The collar tightens only until the smaller loop closes the rings together. The Premier offers the safety of the nylon buckle collars but with the control added by the limited pinching motion.

Harnesses

There are various types of harnesses on the market, including tracking, no-pull, and no-jump harnesses. The no-pull and no-jump harnesses are designed to keep dogs from jumping or pulling by extending under their armpits so that when the dog pulls or jumps, the harness tightens under the forelegs. Although effective in the beginning, dogs can become immune to them quickly. In tracking harnesses, some muscular-chested dogs even pull harder. The goal with any harness is to use it to build a relationship whereby you won't need one.

You can also choose from a variety of head halters. These can be very effective, but can be dangerous if used incorrectly. The concept is based on a horse's halter. Control the head and you can control the dog. The control comes from the increased leverage of moving the collar from the neck to the head. The danger comes from this very same leverage. The possibility for abuse increases as well, as does the risk of neck or head injury to the dog. Horses have longer and stronger necks than dogs. Read the instructions. Watch the videos. If it says to use two leashes, use two leashes. This is a high-potency power tool. It's for a skilled operator.

Leashes

Leashes come in all shapes and sizes, different colors and materials. Nylon is strong, but can be tough on the hands (if you have a pulling dog, train him). Leather is nice and supple but requires periodic care. We like our leashes six feet long, but length is a matter of personal preference. Always make sure you get a leash adequate for the weight of your dog. Make sure the snap is of quality construction (we have seen them break). Also handy are the retractable leashes. These come in different sizes (weight), colors, and lengths. They retract during use, but can lock almost instantly by pushing the thumb button to prevent Thaddeus the Malamute from skidooing.

Electronic Aids

Electronic training aids have become increasingly popular, but they should be used with caution. They shape behavior by administering a correction (usually an electric shock) based on some external stimulus. The aids can be divided into three primary types: invisible fencing, anti-bark collars, and remote-controlled radio collars.

With all of these aids, be aware of the perils of association (see "Watson's Little Albert" in Chapter Four). Your dog may associate the correction with whatever he's reacting to. For example, if your dog runs to the "fence" to bark at kids on bikes, he may relate the resulting shock to kids or bikes and react unpredictably to either in the future.

Invisible fencing won't keep other critters out of your yard and away from your dog. If you decide that invisible fencing is right for you, be sure to buy a system that emits a warning tone prior to applying the correction. As always, do your homework because these devices need to be used appropriately to be safe and effective.

PAWSITIVELY ESSENTIAL EXERCISES

As mentioned, when you bring a new dog home, it's absolutely essential to begin the following training exercises immediately. At the same time, you can go to the other chapters in this section and begin integrating their lessons into your training. In other words, the exercises here and in Chapters Six through Eleven fit together extremely well. You will be pleasantly surprised to discover how easy this is, what a good teacher you are, and how quickly the puppy learns. It does not matter if you are on Week #1 while in Section Two and on Week #2 while in Section Three; merely integrate the two into your daily lifestyle and living arrangements with your pup.

These simple techniques will help to train and desensitize your pup. This will teach him confidence around children and different environments (sights, sounds, and smells). Proceed with each of these exercises one step at a time. Small, successful baby steps are more meaningful and effective than several huge failures. Take a deep breath and please, enjoy the process.

Week #1

Puppy Parties and Socialization

Puppy parties are an enjoyable way to introduce your new addition to people, children, and doorbells. The parties do not have to be elaborate. Gather a few close friends and relatives who enjoy puppies. Have them come over one Sunday afternoon for munchies and a football game. Every time someone arrives, be sure to instruct him or her to have a biscuit and request a "sit" at the front door. You will create a savvy pup that enjoys greeting people at the door without having a conniption.

Introduce your puppy to as many people and other dogs in as many different environments as you possibly can in the first six months. Your best approach when meeting other dogs is to stand back, be calm, have a loose leash, and observe as neutrally as possible. Encourage the pup with a pleasant voice that these are "new friends" and to "go play." You will read a lot more about this throughout the book, but for now, put positive socializing on top of the agenda. The more things that puppies get introduced to, the more confident and friendly they will become.

When meeting people, always try to make it a pleasant experience for the puppy by passing out treats for people to give. Get people to do your homework for you: Show them how to teach "sit," "down," and "stand" so that you can relax. Good places to bring puppies include shopping centers (outside), parks, dog-run parks, play areas, schools (with permission from staff), homes of relatives and friends, training class, hiking, or anywhere else your pup will be accepted and will be offered a positive learning experience.

Bite Inhibition, Part One

In the real world, hands will eventually be near or in your puppy or dog's mouth, whether it be playing with children or on a visit with the veterinarian or groomer. Therefore, it's common sense to teach pups how to bite—softly.

Bite inhibition, or mouthing, is taught in three phases that begin the first day the puppy arrives home. Progress at your own level, as everyone (including the pup) is different, but we highly recommend that you integrate "Bite Inhibition, Part Two" in Week #3, followed by "Bite Inhibition, Part Three" in Week #5. If you go too fast, you may confuse the pup, yet if you proceed too slowly, someone—a child—may get chomped by puppy teeth.

Mouthing

All puppies mouth. It's natural. At about four months, puppies begin a quest for identity by cutting their teeth and your apron strings. You need to teach them the difference between human skin and a chew toy early—at eight weeks of age. When your puppy mouths you, scrunch up your face and dramatically say *"Ouch!"* You do not have to scream, as most pups have extraordinarily good hearing. They will learn more from a change in the muscles in your face, while you say "Ouch!" When the startled pup stops mouthing you and lets go, give her a chew toy. Even better, look for when your pup takes a chew toy independently and snapshot this brilliant act immediately with praise, "Yes" or "Good puppy" (positive reinforcement and behavior shaping).

Encourage mouthing, especially from puppies reluctant to do so. Teach the puppy to bite *softly* before teaching her to stop biting altogether. For a week, try to reduce the number of hard bites only.

Whenever you feel a hard bite, scrunch your face and say "OUCH!" Give the puppy a dirty look. Refuse to play for a few minutes. To really get the point across, leave the room, closing the door behind you to let the puppy consider this turn of events. After a minute or so, make up and resume play. Apply the same reaction to all hard bites until she develops some self-control.

Hand-Feeding of Meals

Now is the age to build up your dog's confidence around the food bowl. You want the puppy to welcome hands near his bowl, not perceive hands as a threatening gesture. We not only want puppies to tolerate human presence around their food dishes, we want them to enjoy us hanging around while they eat. This requires some ingenuity.

Sit next to your puppy's dish. Feed him his meal one kibble at a time. Occasionally, remove the dish. Put in an extra-tasty, healthy morsel. ("A hand taking my dish means a gift.") Every now and then, approach the dish from a distance with a spoonful of low-fat cottage cheese or yogurt. Have children do this, calmly.

Supervise children around dogs and their food bowls, particularly if you have an older dog that you are not sure about. Until you're absolutely comfortable that your dog accepts children around the food bowl, do not take any chances. It's not worth it. Children under the age of 12, unless very precocious and raised with dogs, should not be left unsupervised under any circumstances with dogs, and especially not with strange dogs.

Puppy Push-Ups

Use a food lure (treat or kibble) or toy to maneuver your pup into the sit, down, and stand positions, without touching her. This is a good time to go to Chapter Six, "Lesson Plan: Week #1" for a demonstration of this exercise. As soon as she's getting it, do some with a hand signal only (no food in hand). Praise lavishly, giving the food reward at random from your other hand. When you receive a "sit" or "down" spontaneously, embellish with praise. This creates anticipation and motivates the pup to both sit and down often.

Week #2

Play Doctor

Practice handling your puppy every day. Look into the mouth and ears. Touch her feet, toes, and body. Make it fun. Have others handle the pup. Set boundaries, especially for children (absolutely no rough stuff).

Jolly-Up and Settle-Down

Jolly-up and settle-down are great puppy instructions invented by Dr. Ian Dunbar. It sounds so easy, and it is, but the value of this exercise will make a difference for a lifetime with your dog. The way to *shape* any behavior, and you will hear this over and over again throughout this book, is to *teach* the behavior. The words you use for this exercise are important. We use jolly-up and settle-down, go-play and chill-out, or sparkle and be boring. Dogs will get used to all of them eventually because they have a tremendous repertoire of learning vocabulary.

Every few minutes, while playing with your puppy, have a mandatory time-out period. Call the pup to you at home, in the yard, or in the park. Gently hold her still for 10 seconds or so while telling her "settle-down," "relax," or "chill-out." With repetition, she will start to "settle-down" on request. The key to success here, and with shaping any behavior, is teaching the difference. The difference and the reward here is "go-play" or "jolly-up." Increase the length of the chill-out periods gradually. This works well with high-velocity dogs.

Sit Pronto

Sit is how dogs say please. You can control a sitting dog much easier than one that is leaping. We have never met a dog that can sit and jump at the same time. From now on, the puppy must sit before walks, for greetings, before meals, to go outside, get into the car, and to be allowed to play with dogs or human friends. Don't let her have any of these until she sits. The time to teach basic manners and canine savvy to survive in a human world is now. Sit is a grounding tool that centers you and your dog. On walks, it gives you a moment to take a deep breath, collect your thoughts, and assess a situation before making the next move.

Spook-Proofing

Get your puppy prepared for all the variations of human behavior he may encounter in adult life by doing funny walks. Sing, twirl, skip, and make funny faces while giving a healthy treat. The pup will associate something positive to anything that might appear to be funky or scary. This desensitizing is invaluable and will teach the pup to trust your cues. We integrate this into everyday living experiences and in our training classes by wearing hats, big glasses, and other theatrical attire. We stagger and swing capes over our shoulders. Pop an umbrella open now and again, while smiling and "making nice" to your puppy, of course.

Children are especially good at this, but they can overdo it, too. Acclimate dogs to chaos in a controlled and safe environment with you as leader. Set some boundaries. Again, being a good role model is an essential part of the stages of development for children and pups.

Off-Leash Following

In the first four months, puppies are little balls of cute fluff that follow you everywhere you go. Beyond four months, things can go awry. As mentioned previously, puppies begin cutting teeth and apron strings. They embark into the world to explore new pathways.

Go to a strange, but safe place (far from traffic) for an off-leash walk with your puppy. Walk while encouraging your puppy with your voice or by clapping your hands to follow. Never go after him if he trots off. If he does this, turn and go in the opposite direction, calling him. He doesn't have to follow you precisely, only stay in your general vicinity while exploring his environment. This is a good exercise for teaching your puppy to keep an eye on you.

Flexi leads are a useful tool. They are handheld and reel out and in, so you can give your pup some room without letting him run totally free. If you become concerned about a puppy's explorations (too far and not responding to you when you call) then put him on a Flexi lead.

Week #3

Take-It and Leave-It

Offer your puppy a treat with the invitation to "take-it." Offer another one, but this time tell the pup in a normal tone "leave-it." Close the treat in your hand. When the puppy carries on nuzzling, remind her to "leave-it." Allow her to take it after three seconds or so. Once the concept of "leave-it" is learned, you can use this to teach your pup to leave many other unmentionables.

Grab Desensitization

Eventually, someone will grab your dog. Please begin this exercise gently and slowly. Grab your puppy and give a slight scrunch behind the ear along with a treat. You could also grab the collar. Now, let her go back to what she was doing. After a few times, make a slightly rougher, more abrupt grab. Don't scare the daylights out of her. Gradually, work your puppy up to being relaxed about emergency-level grabs from all directions. This can be useful to desensitize the pup to children grabbing them.

Never grab your puppy or dog by the collar, face, or neck to give a corrective reprimand. What will happen when a child touches the dog around the face or neck area? Hands around the dog's face, whether it is for a hug, a pat on the head, or an examination at the vet's, should be perceived as a nonthreatening gesture for the dog.

Fun Visits

Make a trip to the vet's office, not for shots or treatments, but just to get your puppy used to the place. You can make a lasting impression by making the trip enjoyable for the puppy. Bring extra-special treats for the receptionist to give to the pup. Practice your requests. Show him it's not always a scary place. Do the same at the groomer's or the training location.

Bite Inhibition, Part Two

By now, the puppy may still be mouthing you, but with soft or moderate-pressure bites only because you have been ending play whenever he bites too hard. Now, you're going to pretend the moderate-pressure bites really hurt too. React as in "Bite Inhibition, Part One." Accept very soft bites only. Imitation lambskin toys are excellent for teaching a soft mouth. They also act as a pacifier for puppies and adult dogs who like to hold something in their mouths. It seems to calm them and keeps their mouths off of you.

The Art of Chew-Toy Stuffing

Some of us enjoy a good glass of wine, a movie, popcorn, computer games, sports, or relaxing in a Jacuzzi. Almost all dogs take pleasure in a good chew. Help your puppy develop a pleasant, safe chew-toy habit before she selects other, unacceptable artifacts in your home. One way to get dogs interested in toys is to stuff them. Get a long, sterilized cow bone from a pet store and insert into the middle of the tube a delightful hunk of low-fat cheese or freeze-dried liver. Or, use their kibble. Squeeze cheese and peanut butter work well, too. Have a biscuit sticking out the other end. Some dogs will work for hours to extract the inaccessible morsel in the middle, thus establishing a solid habit. You can also put healthy dog cookies into Kongs, a hollow, hard rubber toy. Smear low-fat peanut butter on the ends of cow bones or Kongs.

Consider the calorie intake when chew-toy stuffing. Dogs need a balanced intake of complex carbohydrates, protein, and fats. They only need as much fuel as energy output. You will need to cut back somewhere if you are chew-toy stuffing. Too confusing or time-consuming? Then simply use their kibble and feed less at dinnertime.

All chew toys should be nonconsumable hard rubber toys.

Week #4

Object Exchanges

With a couple of tasty treats in your hand, walk up to your puppy when she's chewing on a chew toy. Reach for the toy, saying, "Thank you!" Take it away and give the puppy a treat from your hand. Give the toy back. Immediately repeat, saying, "Thank you!" as you remove the toy, and give her another treat. Return the toy to her. Do this a couple of more times. Then leave the puppy to ponder this. Get others to do this, especially children. This builds trust with the puppy.

This exercise is not recommended for adopted dogs until you have carefully assessed their behavior around possessions. This game has to be played fair, as do all of these exercises. Children should be supervised. The object that is taken away should be given back to the dog. Otherwise, what's the point of object exchanges, if the object is taken away and not given back? If a child takes away an object, for example a stuffed dog toy, then scoots in the other direction, a dog with a strong chase (or prey) drive may chase and grab the child or toy.

Hide-and-Seek

An exciting game you can play with your puppy is to hide yourself somewhere in the house. Now call him so he has to look around for you. Some dogs like to look for toys or biscuits. Two people can take turns restraining the dog (gently) while the other one hides. Outside, hide behind trees and bushes. Watch your dog's expressions. It's a hoot. Appreciate the sheer joy that your dog shows when she finds you.

Recalls

Two people can take turns gently holding the dog while the other person practices calling the dog to them from a distance. Do this indoors or in safe outdoor locations. The puppy must sit at the end of each recall to collect his praise, pats, treat, or toy. Doing this in a football field or large area is great exercise. It reinforces the idea that recalls are fun. Allow the puppy to resume playing. Try another recall. You do not want to inadvertently teach him that the moment he comes to you, play is over. It simply means "do this for me now and you get to play again." This is a good family exercise if kept in perspective and under control.

Novel Objects

We have touched on this before, but it's so vital to create an adult dog that's not afraid of his own shadow. Expose your pup to plenty of strange noises and objects, like umbrellas, skateboards, horses, sound-effects tapes (thunder, babies crying, cats meowing), different ethnicities, crowds, glasses, hats, men with beards, and so on. Allow the puppy to approach things at his own speed. Now is the time to get him used to anything he may be exposed to as an adult. If your pup seems sound shy or has trouble focusing on objects, speak to your veterinarian.

Week #5

Fun Rollovers

Desensitize your puppy slowly to strange things, smells, sounds, and sights by associating these stimuli with a pleasant experience. Don't kid yourself into thinking that a dog will perceive you as a wolf or alpha dog if you use a rollover or a good hard stare in the eyeballs for corrections. This can be treacherous if tried by a child. Dogs know instinctively that humans are not dogs.

Instead, teach your dog to like rough personhandling within reason. Most dogs will receive this from children anyway. Don't do this exercise if you haven't first practiced grabbing or are unclear as to what this means (see "Grab Desensitization" in Week #3). Roll him onto his back. Give him a treat and tummy rub. Let the pup know that you are in control whether the situation is chaotic or not.

Greeting Rituals

The previously described Puppy Parties are great for this too. Take a walk around the block. Have two or three friends walk around the same block, separately in the opposite direction, so that you will meet one of them every couple of minutes. Each time you meet one, instruct the puppy to sit, have your accomplice greet the puppy after she sits, and then carry on. Do several sit greetings with each person. Repeat this exercise with different accomplices. Practice this at the front door with friends, letter carriers, or the UPS delivery person.

Bite Inhibition, Part Three

If your puppy has been consistently applying only very low-pressure bites, you may now forbid biting altogether. Start reacting to all bites. Teach him that he may bite the toys and treats you offer ("take-it") but that he may never mouth you unless you invite him to do so. You must selectively eliminate the harder bites before you try to eliminate all bites. This teaches bite inhibition.

TRAINING TIPS

As you work through the Pawsitively Essential exercises, keep the Four D's in mind:

Delivery. Very early on in the training process you will want to randomize the delivery of your reward. Otherwise, reward-giving loses momentum. Start to reward only the very best behavior, or desired sequence of behavior, with a jackpot treat. For example: Sit, down, stay for 10 seconds. If you're changing another "D" criteria, you may want to go back to delivering the rewards more often. If you are teaching something new, then by all means reward the desired response.

Distance. Increase distance gradually. Increasing too quickly may cause the dog to make a mistake like breaking a sit-stay. The dog comes when called while on a six-foot lead. Great! Now try a Flexi lead or longer rope at 10 feet. Go off lead only in safe places and when you are sure your dog will come to you.

Duration. The dog is steady on her sit-stay for five seconds, then 10 seconds. Try extending the exercise to 15 seconds, then one minute.

Diversity. The dog performs well in her usual, calm training environment (home, yard, and classroom). Now it's time to complicate matters a little by introducing distractions. Take her to a new site that is distracting just because it's new. Will she walk as nicely on a loose leash in the park as she does in the backyard? Will she sit-stay in your living room if you walk to the closet and put on your coat? Will she come if called while the doorbell is ringing? This is a challenge. Will she "shush" when the doorbell is ringing, because you said "thank you for alerting, now quiet"?

How Effective Is Your Praise?

Most dogs will gleefully wait in anticipation for what the outcome of a response will be to your request. You can maximize the response you get for praise, treats, or any other life reward by answering these questions:

1. Does your form of praise (other than food) result in your dog's greater effort to please you? If so, then you are effectively using variable reinforcement using treats intermittently, or not at all. You have discovered other life rewards to grab your dog's undivided attention. You know what motivates him or her to take the challenge.

2. Can you name two favorite spots to scratch that bring the same results as the best tidbit, treat, or toy?

3. What voice inflection or pitch brings about the best response in your dog?

4. How do you convince your dog that you are really, really pleased with her performance?

5. How does your dog tell you that she feels praised enough to be pleased with herself (for example, awareness of body language, little noises in the back of her throat, lifted her front leg for a scratch, devoted look in her eyes, and so on).

6. What words do you use when giving praise? Are they always the same? Are you boring and losing momentum in your training plan? Are you challenging your dog or doing the same repeated exercises over and over ad nauseam? Are you challenging yourself with your dog by taking a bit of risk every now and then (trying something new)? Are you being creative with games?

And how effective is your message of correction? Instead of "No, no bad dog" or "Shame, shame," try "Ackk," "Too bad," "So sad," "Tough luck (!#$?)." Stick your tongue out at him or simply walk away. Turning your back to a dog is a total insult. It usually leaves them pondering (in a dog's way). Always return and resume your activity after a few minutes. The idea is to teach the dog your language and guidelines in English and in a way that he understands. You need to use your body language, ingenuity, and practice the techniques offered here to do this effectively.

Other Ways to Praise

Here are some alternatives to the same old boring "Good boy" or "Good girl":

- Bravo
- OK
- Excellent
- Outstanding
- Awesome
- Wahoo
- Yes
- Clever
- Delightful
- Delirious
- Alright
- Wonderful
- Marvelous
- Magnificent
- Great
- Hot Dog

Common Training Questions

Here are some common questions that may arise as you train your dog:

What if my dog doesn't like treats or won't work for food?
Hee, hee, that's laughable! This makes us chuckle because every dog eats or it'd be dead. The trick is to use a preferred, delicious food and

train when the dog is hungry, not full. Keep in mind what you have learned about variable reinforcement and momentum. A full dog isn't interested in more food, unless it is leading a boring life.

What if I have more than one dog?
So what? Separate the dogs. Work with one at a time for 10- or 15-minute sessions. The other dogs may hear the clicks or enthusiastic praise, but they won't receive the treats or your company, which is special to them. They won't be confused, just eager for their turn. The alternative: Work with them all together, if you dare.

How long should a training session be? How often should I train?
Five-minute to 10-minute sessions, whenever you can and depending on the dog's enthusiasm and willingness to perform. More and longer is not better. Short training bursts/sessions are more fun, rewarding, and less tiring than long, drawn-out ceremonious events. Quality always outweighs quantity.

Should I train more than one behavior at a time?
Sure, but do not work on more than one detail of any given behavior at a time. For example, if you are working on getting your dog to wag her tail, then praise or treat for tail wagging. Work on sit-stay or down separately, unless she is sitting and her tail happens to start wagging. Snapshot the wag, then add on your cue. Chances are your dog may automatically sit anyway while wagging because most dogs have learned to sit first.

What happens if I make a mistake?
If you don't, we are very concerned because we all make mistakes. Laugh it off. Play with your dog. It's easy to click or praise too soon, too late, or too many times. When we learn something new, we all get excited. Lock yourself in a room and have a clicking party with yourself. Remember, training is fun, fair, flexible, and forgiving for everyone. No damage is done as long as you are aware of what you are doing.

What do I do if my dog makes a mistake?
Shoot him—just kidding. Checking to see if you are conscious. Simply, don't click or praise. Don't say "no" or "stupid idiot" or jerk the leash. It will only make the dog less interested in training. Just say, "Tisk, tisk, too bad, what a pity, tough luck." Then try again later, or do something that they are good at and click or praise and treat.

Think about what it would be like to come home with A's and B's on a report card and have your parent say, "Oh, the A's are good, maybe you can improve the B's." This is clearly not a self-esteem enhancer and wouldn't motivate many of us to try harder. It's the same for dogs. If they try and try again, without reward, they'll give up or keep making mistakes to get attention. You lose momentum, relationship steps, and their respect. How sad and foolish. All that hard work down the drain because of our human egos.

A well-trained Dalmatian maintains eye contact while walking. Positive reinforcement creates a dog that is doing things for you because he wants to, which makes everyone happy. (Photo by Winter-Churchill Photography)

Does that mean I should never punish my dog?

That depends on how you define punishment. To be successful, punishment must be absolute, quick, and used every time for that misbehavior. It's an impossible task, so it is doomed to failure. Punishment will temporarily cease a behavior in your presence, that's it. The behavior will likely reoccur, like a rash every time you step into poison ivy. The solution is to teach. When you scold (corrective reprimand) to stop a behavior, or better still, express your displeasure by either ignoring it or walking away disgusted, follow up by teaching the preferred behavior.

This can be as simple as picking up all of the toys or training equipment and walking away. The likelihood is that your dog will ponder on this, then follow you. Seize the moment with an exercise they do well and praise. Continue on this positive learning path.

Shouldn't the dog respect, even fear me, to ensure long-term reliability?

True reliability is earned with respect and trust whether from a dog or human. Reinforcement creates a dog that is doing things for you because he wants to; he understands what his job is to keep you happy and thereby get what he wants to keep him happy.

When do I use commands or requests?

When the dog has learned the behavior. Add, "sit." The dog now gets a click or praise and treat only after you say "sit" and she sits. This sounds complicated, but it really isn't. As you integrate the day-to-day lessons from Section Three, you will see that you can teach your eight-week-old puppy to sit-down-and-sit and stand-down-and-stay with a food lure in about five minutes without giving it a name. The sit, down, stand, stay, and come will be piggybacked onto the behavior after you teach the behavior. We have found that it works either way, so don't worry about it if you give it a name like "sit" from the get-go or decide to teach the behavior and tack the cue on later. It's a habit for most of us anyway. We are more comfortable holding the treat and saying "sit" at the same time. That is equally as effective, and in some respects, takes less time. Dogs are clever and will get the message either way.

What if you give a cue and the dog doesn't do it?

How is your dog feeling today? Seriously, dogs have their good days and their bad days just like us humans. Do you have the dog's attention? Those concerns aside, then you have not established the cue under that circumstance. A dog may sit beautifully at home, but would rather chase squirrels at the park. You need to introduce training with distractions under new conditions such as a park, the beach, in front of a store, in parking lots, at malls, and so forth.

When can I get rid of food?

Once the behavior is really learned, technically, you will not need the treat, but it's still nice to give it to him once in a while simply because he loves the treat and you love your dog. Depending on the dog, and your training skills, by two years of age most dogs will sit, stay, down, get off the couch, and go for walks without treats. There are certainly dogs that achieve this level sooner, especially when variable reinforcement is used (treats given intermittently and not every single time the behavior is accomplished). Remember, what you are trying to accomplish is to teach a single, or new behavior, then increase this to a series of behaviors (known as chaining) before rewarding. When you decide to teach a new behavior or your dog is bored with your repertoire, break out the clicker and treats, and your best praise voice (or favorite dog motivator) and begin again.

Chapter Six

Lesson Plan: Week #1

Socialization should be one of the first items on your training agenda. Pups need to be exposed to anything they will be exposed to as an adult, such as a variety of environments, people, children, and other dogs. Puppies will grow to be confident and savvy adult dogs who like people and usually other dogs. Learning the basic guidelines in this week's lesson will make socialization much easier for you and your puppy (or dog).

THE COLLAR AND LEASH

Any collar you choose to use should fit the pup gently and properly. Choker chains, for example, are not recommended for puppies and dogs with large heads. People tend to buy the chain in an enormous size to fit over the dog's head. When the chain is lax, it falls around the chest area, which happens to be the most muscular area for most dogs. Imagine trying to train a Husky or Rottweiler to walk on a loose leash using an oversized choker chain—you're setting yourself up for failure, as the dog will win, strengthwise, every time. Another point to ponder: Is this really the kind of relationship training you want to develop with your puppy or adult dog? Pull, tug, jerk, and get pulled forward, then maybe fall down? Doesn't sound like fun to us. We've been there, done that, and we suggest the easy, gentler approach that will keep both you and your dog free of scrapes and bruises. So, pick a collar that makes sense, whether it be buckle or adjustable. Use your brain and behavior shaping, not brawn and heavy-duty equipment to build a healthy training relationship with your dog.

We recommend and use Premier adjustable collars. You can locate others that are similar. The design is a martingale-style collar with a handhold that adjusts as the puppy grows (which is cost effective). Most importantly, they're gentle on a growing puppy's neck. An added perk is that the handhold is helpful in traffic, in pet-therapy work, and for desensitizing puppies to hands around the neck and head. They're easier to use for older adults or people who might have a more difficult time holding the collar.

Remember what we emphasized before? Touch the collar often, but touch it in a positive way. If you grab the handhold or any other collar of a dog for correction or to yank him around, you are setting a precedent. The dog will dislike and perhaps fear hands around his neck and face—not a good thing for a dog living with children who poke, probe, and hug on a regular basis.

Maureen shows how to touch the collar in positive way.
Remember: Touch collar. Praise!
(Photo by Gary Ross)

Here's how to fit and use the collar:

1. Put your collar of choice on your dog (not you). If you are using Premier, or something similar, gently slide the larger loop part of the collar over the dog's head.

2. Adjust so that the O-rings almost touch directly behind the dog's ears when the collar is tightened with leash or hand.

3. Adjust the collar (slide-ring) to fit the dog's neck comfortably.

4. Attach leash to the larger round ring between the two O-rings.

5. Loosen the collar to adjust size, as needed (e.g., when the puppy grows).

To achieve a comfortable control position with the leash, follow these procedures:

1. Put your right thumb through the loop of the leash, or just hold it comfortably without wrapping it around your hand and arms.

2. Fold the excess back and forth "accordion-style" into your right hand, leaving enough slack to create the letter "J."

3. Place your right hand, palm down, in front of your right leg.

4. Grasp the leash with your left hand, palm down, in front of your left leg.

You may be asking yourself, "What's the big deal with the leash?" None really, except for form and to make it less cumbersome for you. If you are holding onto it, that is the most important criterion here. You do not need to be focusing on excess leash hanging everywhere, but you do need a six-foot leash to give your dog some slack, and thus teach the basics of walk-on-a-loose-leash. If you are using a traffic leash (about two to three feet long), then what choices do you and your dog have?

BASIC COMMANDS

Now let's tackle the basic commands: heel, sit, down, stand, and come.

Heel Position and Walk-on-a-Loose-Leash

Heel position is when your dog is facing in the same direction you are, lined up on your left side (or right, if you prefer) next to your hip. Walk-on-a-loose-leash is simply walking without the dog pulling on the leash. It's a relaxed walk where there's slack on the leash, but you have a choice about where your dog is (front, side, a little behind).

Using Food Lures and Rewards

Using food lures is a way to get your pup's attention focused on you. It's not a bribe especially, as she will get fed anyway. It's an unconditional reinforcer. Food is an effective incentive for training. It gives you the ability to not only get your dog's attention but also to do so quickly. It motivates her response to a request. Food communicates pleasure, so the dog will associate training with pleasure. Tennis balls, squeaky toys, clapping hands, and clicking (whatever works) can be used as attention getters and motivators. Reminder: Food lures are small, *healthy* treats that will later be used at variable intervals. You can use your dog's dry kibble. It helps to avoid feeding your dog full meals before training or the food lure will lose its appeal swiftly.

Maureen uses a food lure to get the attention of two puppies.
(Photo by Gary Ross)

The secret to success here is easy to find. You do not even need to worry yet about using cues like sit, down, stand, or stay. The exciting part of this is that you can teach sit, down, stand, stay, or any other behavior by first getting the behavior, then praising and treating it. In other words, if you weren't able to speak, you could still train your dog.

Words for each behavior can come later (in the next lesson). If you're eager, like we usually are, we add the word right along with the food luring, eye contact, and teaching the basic foundation that dogs need to learn for living comfortably in a human world. We find that families and individuals with busy lifestyles, or people who get bored easily, cannot do this in slow motion. It's up to you how much gusto you put into this. We do not believe that there's any real magic to doing this one way or the other, just do it. If you are getting the results you like, then you are on the right track.

Sit

Remember to shape the behaviors you want. Catch your dog in the act of doing something right. So watch for automatic sits, and then praise the dog. To teach the sit with dog standing and the food lure in your right hand, palm upwards, slowly move the lure up and over the dog's head, then wiggle it so he looks up and back. Continue to move the food lure back over the muzzle until the dog sits. Anatomically, the dog has to sit. Try this little posture yourself. Stand up, touch the ground with your hands if you can, then try to look at the sky. You have to bring your derriere down. Good. Your dog is sitting. Now touch the collar, praise and reward with a treat/motivator. Later on, add your cue "sit" prior to the lure.

Attention Game

Lure your puppy into a sit with a food treat. Bring the treat next to your face to get the pup's attention. When the puppy looks at you, praise and treat. Next time, wait three seconds, then five, then eight, and so forth. Add a cue, like, "Watch me." Any time the puppy looks at you willingly, praise and treat because you want the pup to rely on you for what's coming next (eager anticipation).

In this sequence, Maureen achieves a sit by using a food lure.
(Photos by Gary Ross)

Down

With your dog sitting, a food lure in your right hand, and your palm downwards, quickly move the lure in front of the dog's eyes. It works best if the lure is close and under the dog's muzzle. Otherwise, you will find (and this has happened hundreds of times) that your dog will stand instead of down. You have pulled the food lure out and forward instead of down. Be vigilant and patient. Don't give up. Bring that food lure to the floor or the ground right under the muzzle. Lower it directly down in-between the paws. Hold it there. Talk encouragingly. Be patient.Keep trying. The dog will soon lie down. Touch the collar. Give praise, reward. When you are comfortable with this, add your cue, "Down."

Alternate Hands-On Techniques for Down

We offer alternative hands-on or physical prompt techniques to students. Some dogs will not respond to a down with the food-lure approach. Some are simply too clever or receive food and treats often, so there is no real desire. When you consider survival or pack leadership, down isn't exactly a great place to be for a dog unless he is confident in his position within the pack (human or otherwise). With your help, dogs can learn that it can be a safe place and exciting place to be because "good things happen when I'm down."

In this sequence, Maureen achieves a down by moving the food lure to the ground right under the dog's muzzle. (Photos by Gary Ross)

You can teach the down by gently leaning over the dog and sliding out his front paws. If your dog is in a sit position, think about the foundation of an "A" frame. If you pick up one leg, and gently push the dog toward that same side, he will slide into a down. You can sit on the floor or ground and lure your dog under one leg. This exercise is challenging with giant breeds.

Stand

Stand is an invaluable position for your dog on visits to the vet or the groomer. It can be useful for grooming at home. With the dog sitting, the food lure in your right hand, move the lure forward away from the dog's nose, parallel to the ground. The dog will follow and stand. Reinforce with touching the collar, praise, and then reward. Then add in your cue, "Stand."

An alternate stand technique is to use your six-foot leash. Bring the loop end down and under the dog's belly, then up to the other side. You now have something that looks like a handle on a basket to hold your dog in a stand position.

Come

Kneel, or bend over, and clap your hands to get your dog's attention, call "come" with lots of enthusiasm. Praise and reward with food (or other motivational pleasure, such as toys). Practice in the house with your dog out of sight or asleep. Repeat as often as possible without causing unnecessary stress. This is important: *Get your dog coming to you at all times, in different locations and under varied circumstances.* Remember what we advised about come on recall: Never call your dog to you for a corrective reprimand or punishment. It's counterproductive. Go to your dog for reprimands, then teach the desired behavior.

Note: This is an effective way of integrating the use of hand and voice signals. It provides alternative ways of communicating. If the dog's eyesight or hearing diminishes with age, you will always have another means of signaling your dog.

Holding the food lure in her right hand, Maureen achieves a stand by moving it forward away from Sage's nose, parallel to the ground.
(Photo by Gary Ross)

HOMEWORK

Sorry, but some things will always be the same. Practice makes perfect. Integrate training into your daily regimen and lifestyle with your dog. Remember, "You do something for me and I'll do something for you." If you slack off, and your dog becomes destructive or engages in other behaviors that really make your hair stand on end, then guess what? You have to take accountability for it and get back in the groove.

You should set aside 10 to 15 minutes twice a day for formal sessions, with many informal and fun sessions as an integral part of daily living. Practice each of the following:

1. Sit-down-sit and stand-down-stand: Five times each exercise, twice daily (try doing this at the food bowl or when waiting to go out the door).

2. Come: Several times a day (with the family).

3. Attention-getting "Watch me": Lots of these this week.

4. Play after each training session. Keep it fun; always end with a success.

Chapter Seven

Lesson Plan: Week #2

As always and for all species, the learning process is on a continuum. As mentioned in the beginning of *Train Your Dog, Change Your Life*, we recommend using the whole book while focusing on these lessons regularly. Chapter Five, "Basic Training for Puppies," should be a part of your daily repertoire, as well.

You will reach some highs and lows in the training process. Prepare to experience some spectacular plateaus when your puppy, or dog, just does it naturally. Catch these special learning moments and lock them in with praise. You may also come across some impasses in training. Don't sweat them and do not take them personally. Puppies and dogs have their days, just like humans. It will all come together naturally if you persist. We all need a jumpstart or refresher course every now and then, and so do dogs.

We strongly encourage you to focus on the behaviors you want and snapshot those behaviors pronto. Look for that automatic sit or down, or a gentle touch to your child's hand. When this is offered spontaneously, praise that behavior without hesitation. Work smart, not hard ... life is way too short. Okay, let's continue on from Week #1.

Be mindful that you have a choice to practice whatever exercise you want to with your dog, but consistency, particularly in the beginning stages of training, will help the dog, especially puppies, focus better on you and what you are teaching (e.g., sit-down-and-sit or walk-on-a-loose-leash).

HEEL (DOG ALIGNED AT YOUR LEFT HIP)

Begin with a your puppy in a sit position by your side. Using a food lure or your voice, walk to entice your dog to be by your side. Use your voice or whatever works to gain attention.

Maureen uses a food lure and her voice to encourage Sage to heel.
(Photo by Gary Ross)

WALK ON A LOOSE LEASH
(DOG WALKING WITHOUT PULLING)

Whenever the dog pulls on the leash, turn in the opposite direction and play "catch-up" by calling the dog. Praise and reward whenever the dog is in a satisfactory position. An alternative technique is to practice Zen: Be a tree. When the dog pulls on the leash, stand still and stay calm until the dog returns to an acceptable position or loosens the leash. Praise lavishly and reward by continuing the walk.

Use common sense when taking your dog for a walk. If your dog has been confined for several hours, she will undoubtedly have an enormous amount of energy to release. Give her and yourself time to release it, then go for your walk. Then begin your training sessions.

Maureen and Sage show how to execute a loose-leash walk.
(Photo by Gary Ross)

ABOUT-TURN

About-turns are used to reverse directions while walking, keeping your dog by your side, and paying attention. Turn in place to your right (dog on the outside) and continue heeling. This teaches the dog to keep his eye on you: The message communicated to the dog is, "Hello, where am I? Watch for me." If you read "Cross Training" in Chapter Fifteen, then now is the time to incorporate a little bit of creativity. Make good use of bushes, trees, poles, and people, while being mindful of your dog's age and level of progress. Puppies really need some focus, so it's best to begin slowly and quietly. A training class can be a pretty noisy place at times, but you can practice quietly, in short sessions, with your pup at home until she gets the concept of what you're teaching.

AUTOMATIC SITS

Sitting solves jumping and countertop theft. A dog that sits or downs respectfully in the kitchen and during dinners is one that's welcomed in the house. If you catch your dog before he enjoys his first turkey-grab off the counter, then you are in good training shape. Have your dog sit or lie down in the kitchen, around countertops and tables, and during dinnertime. Teach him to go to his mat. No time? Okay, then let him enjoy crate haven for a while. (See "Crate Haven" in Chapter Twelve.) If you like doling out healthy tidbits, so be it, but always ask for something first like a sit or down.

With your dog walking by your side and a food lure in your right hand, halt. Before halting, it's recommended that you slow your walk a bit, then halt. This gives the dog a cue ("Okay, my owner is slowing down, so usually the next movement is stop"). Move the food lure up and over the dog's head quickly, so he looks up and back. Cue "sit." Praise and reward if you received a prompt sit. If not, oh well, try again.

SIT, DOWN, STAND

Continue as in Week #1, but keep the dog on your left side, instead of in front of you. Sit-down-and-sit and stand-down-and-stand. Your dog quickly learns to watch for your hand, which will provide your hand signals. You should be good at this by now. Food-lure hand movements become effective hand signals. You can use a ball, a squeaky toy, or any other motivator, too.

COME

Continue training informally indoors as in Week #1. To enhance real-life training from this point on, always ask for a sit when in front of a human. A sitting dog cannot jump on you. Practice your sits, and then, when you call your dog to you, have her sit. Praise and reward. Ensure and enforce this same technique with family and friends. When you're out for a walk in a park, have people who want to meet, greet, and pet your dog request a sit first.

Take your dog outdoors on a long leash or Flexi lead. When your dog is *not* paying attention, call "come" and skip (or walk) in the opposite direction. Kneel or clap using a cheerful voice. Do whatever is necessary, but get your dog to come. Convince your dog it is relevant to be with you. Praise and reward.

STAY

Your dog is sitting in heel position or comfortably by your side. Hold the leash in your left hand over the dog's head. With your right hand, wave from right to left across the front of the dog's muzzle and say, "stay." In other words, just put your hand out flat, palm exposed toward your dog's muzzle. Turn directly in front of the dog so that you are toe to toe. Reinforce after 10 seconds, then 20 seconds, and work your way up to one minute. Praise and reward. This same hand signal for stay can be used from afar; you will simply change your body position from the side to the front, further away, then hold your palm in front of the dog while saying, "stay." Remember that if you get overzealous and work too fast, your dog will have a brain cramp and make a mistake. It makes more sense to begin slowly, constantly reinforcing the correct behavior. Then, expand your time and proximity away from your dog. Walk away, and come back in, but continually reinforce the behavior you want: sit-stay.

To achieve a sit-stay, Maureen puts out her palm, flat and exposed; towards the dog's muzzle. (Photo by Gary Ross)

TAKE-IT AND LEAVE-IT

Using a food lure, voice, and/or hand signal, position your dog into a sit-stay. Hold treats in your open hand several inches away from the dog's muzzle and say, "leave-it." Close your hand promptly if the dog lunges for the treat. Puppies will! Repeat until the dog stops lunging. Hold for three to five seconds. Say "take-it" and let the dog have the treat. Praise. Repeat exercise.

Gary asks Casidy to "leave-it" (left) and"take-it" (right). (Photo by Maureen Ross)

Alternative exercise: Have your dog sit-stay. Put the food about one foot away on the floor or ground with your foot positioned over it, and say, "leave-it." If your dog lunges for the treat, no problem; simply put your foot down over it (without squashing it) and say, "leave-it!" Repeat as above. Wait a few seconds: Okay, take-it, and praise and reward.

Timing

Important: *Do not allow the dog to move.* If the dog moves, immediately put him back into a sit-stay position. Timing with quick corrections followed by praise is most effective. Practice stay five times per session. Add on take-it and leave-it. Take-it is a good request for retrieving, too. Leave-it is a good request for many reasons: on walks, with other dogs, with people, and other unmentionables; basically anything you prefer your dog to leave alone.

GAMES

Eye-to-Eye Contact: Attention-Getting Game

As mentioned several times throughout *Train Your Dog, Change Your Life*, before you can teach your dog anything, it's necessary to get the dog's attention. Using your tone of voice, food lures, and/or a squeaky toy — whatever works — say to your dog, "Look at me" or "Watch me." Try to capture *true* eye contact for three to five seconds. Praise and reward.

Jolly-Up and Settle-Down (Dr. Dunbar's Good-Manners Game)

There's nothing more pleasing than to have a well-mannered canine companion. You can accomplish this by playing jolly-up and settle-down games. Using your voice and body language, jolly-up your dog by saying, "Come on — let's play, Sparkle!" or "Come on — let's dance!" When your dog is excited, say in a calm but meaningful voice, "Okay, settle-down," or "Go to your mat." Now, have your dog sit or down. If he cooperates, praise and reward. This teaches your dog that not only is play fun, but settling down is rewarding, too.

HOMEWORK

You should set aside 10 minutes, twice a day, for formal training, with as many informal training sessions as possible integrated into everyday living and learning. Practice each of the following:

1. Heeling/Walk-on-a-loose-leash: Five to ten minutes per day, or more.

2. Attention-getting game: As often as possible.

3. Sit-down-and-sit, stand-down-and-stand: Five times each, twice daily.

4. Sit-stay: Three times, twice daily.

5. Take-it, leave-it: As often as you choose.

6. Come: Practice as often as possible (inside and outside).

7. Play sessions are important after training. This creates a positive association.

8. Focus on using one request at a time, and be sure that your dog associates it with the requested behavior. Multiple requests are confusing (a dog cannot sit and down at the same time).

9. Have a pawsitive attitude. Don't train when you are in a bad mood.

10. Visualize your canine companion responding to your every expectation.

11. KISS (Keep It Short, Silly). Sure, kiss and hug your dog. It's therapeutic! Your goal is to have a reliable dog who trusts you — a relationship is based on mutual respect.

12. Request, Response, Reward, Respect: A reminder about the four R's that will help making training easier and more memorable.

Chapter Eight

Lesson Plan: Week #3

PHASING OUT FOOD REWARDS

Here's where we begin to use variable reinforcement schedules (treating at intervals for desired sequences of behavior). Puppies are relatively easy to train. They're exuberant and willing do anything for the sake of doing it, especially for a treat. When they reach adolescence, they begin to ask, "Why should I do this?" This is when you may see your six-month-old look at you upon your request to "Come here, Sage" and then find her wandering in the opposite direction. You've lost your touch and charisma. Go back to teaching her the relevance of responding to your request. We call it, "You do something for me, and I'll do something for you." With older dogs, "jumpstarting" is a good way of looking at it when training has lost its momentum.

The rewards you give your dog should equal the quality of the response. If she responds to your request in a way that you deem spectacular, then by all means give her the jackpot (treat, praise, play ball). If she offers you a blasé response, reflect on how you are feeling about training your dog because this usually mimics the response you get. Ensure she's feeling well today. How's the weather? Too hot, maybe? These factors all affect your training sessions. Have you had a chance lately to play or take a walk so your dog can simply have a good sniff, or are you getting a bit too regimented with your training protocol? Are you, the children, relatives, or friends doling out treats for the heck of it? If they are, then you know by now that this is going to put a damper on your training sessions. Your dog thinks, "Why work if I can get my lunch for free?" Are you consciously present while you are training? You get the picture.

To sharpen up your exercises and the dog's response to your training, you must not let treating or praise lose momentum. It will if you continue treating or praising every single little thing that your dog does. You need to begin asking for a little more. The dog doesn't have to go off to search and find a missing person, but he does need to give you more than a half-hearted sit before receiving a positive life reward from you.

Integrate the sit, stay, down, and stand into everyday living situations. For example, "sit" before greeting people, getting supper, coming inside, going outside, putting on leash, getting into car, getting massaged, throwing a tennis ball, or cuddling on the couch. The dog learns the cues of what behaviors will get him what he wants. They are good at the game, so teach them how to play fairly. No free lunch.

DIRECTIONAL HEELING/CIRCLE LEFT, RIGHT

Begin in a comfortable, controlled position, give the request, and make a circle to the left. At the end of each circle, your dog should sit. This may seem boring, but it's significant to teach your dog to follow your direction. Circle right: Same as above but make a few circles to the right. Go bush hunting. When you find some interesting bushes and shrubs on walks, intermittently circle and weave around them.

SIT-STAY

Place the rings of the collar and snap of the leash under your dog's chin. With the dog sitting in heel position, give the stay request with your right hand, walk three feet, pivot, and face your dog. Keep the dog in sit-stay for up to one minute. Return to your dog with your right hand holding the lead, slide your left hand down the lead, walk to the right and back around the rear of the dog to the heel position. You are in effect making a circle around your dog. The dog must remain in the sit-stay. If your dog moves, reposition and repeat the exercise. Have you noticed that you are now increasing your distance away from your dog as you circle around the back of him? This is excellent, but do it wisely. Walk a few feet to the right first, reinforce the stay, then walk towards the back, reinforce and so on. You get the picture. Most dogs will follow you around the circle if you don't go slowly. What you are accomplishing by doing this is teaching him that no matter where you ask for a sit-stay (any position), if he just stays there, you'll be right back. Praise and reward.

Gary uses a hand signal to keep Casidy in a sit-stay. (Photo by Maureen Ross)

DOWN

Give your dog the down request—same as last week. After the dog is down, give the stay request. Stand at the dog's side for up to about a minute. You can integrate the same circle around the back of your dog as in the sit-stay. If your dog begins to get up, simply reinforce the down-stay. Make a half-circle the first time, or just take a few steps to the right. That's good enough at this point. If you can make the complete circle, without your dog moving, great! Praise and reward.

LONG DOWN

This is a tough one that we always hear someone balk at. We highly encourage you to follow through with this exercise. It makes a huge dif-ference between having a dog that can stay calmly in the house when family, friends, or relatives are visiting to having a dog that you relegate to the basement, crate, or backyard because of rowdy behavior.

Practice three times. Starting with you sitting next to your dog, place the dog into a down and enforce for 30 minutes. That's right— 30 minutes! This teaches control and reinforces the down request. This is easier to accomplish while watching TV, reading a book, or listening to music. Children will have to comply and be supervised because it's unfair to have the children bouncing around while you are trying to teach the dog to down-stay and be calm for 30 minutes.

If you follow through persistently, the outcome, pretty close to 90 percent of the time, will be that the dog falls asleep or calms down. When he wakes up, or when the 30 minutes are over, praise lavishly and reward. Again, be savvy and pick an opportune time to do this. After the puppy has been fed, given the chance to eliminate, and exercised— this is a good time to settle-down for 30 minutes. Take a deep breath.

COME-ON-RECALL

Place your dog in a sit-stay and drop the leash. Walk 10 feet, turn and face your dog. Pause, kneel (unless this is an uncomfortable position for you), pause again, open your arms, and call your dog while praising liberally. Continue to use food rewards intermittently for recalls by first showing the treasured treat to them, then walking away with the treasure. If you receive an enthusiastic, almost knock-you-down come-on-recall, then jackpot! Remember to request a sit, so the dog does not actually knock you down. Always, always praise and reward a dog that comes to you willingly and jackpot a dog that zips to you enthusiastically and sits automatically in front of you, or even diagonally. It doesn't matter, unless you are in obedience competition trials, if your dog sits like a marine or not. Just get the dog to sit in front of humans. Have them say, "Please." The "Jumping" section in Chapter Fourteen helps you learn how to teach your dog the up and off commands. If you desire to have a dog jump up to greet you, teach him the difference. It saves a lot of heartache later on. He should always come to you, his friend and leader, with a positive and safe greeting, one with understanding and clear expectations.

In this sequence, Maureen demonstrates
a come-on-recall. "Sit."

"Stay."

"Come."

Casidy comes.

"What a good dog!"

HOMEWORK

You should set aside at least 10 to 15 minutes, twice a day, for formal training, with as many informal training sessions as possible integrated into everyday living and learning. Practice each of the following:

1. Long 30-minute down; try to do this at least three times this week.

2. Stay, stand, down, twice daily.

3. Sit, stay, then a down, stay for one minute, and add in a circle finish around your dog.

4. Sit-stay, take-it, leave-it.

5. Heel or walk-on-a-loose-leash at least 10 minutes per day.

6. Recall five times daily.

7. Keep it pawsitive. Play during and after training.

8. Continue eye-contact game, jolly-ups, and settle-downs for the rest of your life.

Chapter Nine

Lesson Plan: Week #4

HEEL OR WALK-ON-A-LOOSE-LEASH

Taking your dog for a walk should be a pleasure, not a pain. Your dog will respond more rapidly to training if she associates it with the anticipation of a delightful experience like long walks to the park, free-running exercise in a fenced area, playing retrieve or hide-and-seek games. By Week #4, your teammate should have a pretty good understanding that a walk will happen if she is by your side and not pulling. Continue with this process forever; it never ends. Like conditioning muscles, it improves with repetitions.

In this sequence, Maureen leads Casidy in a heel with loose leash.

An alternative approach to correct lunging or lagging is simply to turn in the opposite direction. When your dog is where you want her, then mark this with praise. Zen: Be a tree. Don't move until your dog is by your side.

CHANGING PACE AND SAVING FACE

Practice changing pace frequently: Normal, slow, normal, fast, normal, skip, jog, or hop on one foot (it's your prerogative). This may seem boring or silly, but it teaches the dog to pay attention and follow your direction. It also continually desensitizes the dog to what he is bound to see in real life. Be creative: Weave around bushes or cars in a parking lot. Change the flow of directions often. Do a reality walk. Stop, sit down at the park, tell your dog it's time to meditate or whatever suits your fancy, and take a few moments to be in the present. Continuously encourage your dog when you get the behavior that you want. Say "quickly" for speeding up, or "easy" for slowing the pace, or "gently" for a light touch, or "quietly" for a peaceful moment. The words aren't as relevant as the timing and cues. Know that your dog lives by associations, and if you have a mutual respect for one another, he will generally follow your cues. He will learn by looking for cues, then receiving consequences for behaviors he performs—whether good or bad.

DISTANCE AND DISTRACTIONS

It's time to challenge your skills by adding some more distance (i.e., sit-stay at six feet, farther, and so on). With your dog in a sit-stay, walk to the end of the lead. Wait a few seconds. Walk back in to reinforce with a treat or scratch. Do several of these. Begin to increase your distance. Remember, if your dog makes the mistake of moving from a sit, it's because he has associated with some cue to move or still doesn't know what sit is. So, regress. That's okay. Begin with basic sits and downs as a refresher.

Remember how keen your dog's senses are: sight, hearing, olfactory. Your dog could be viewing and focusing on some very minute movement, like a twitch of your finger, to respond to a come-on-recall. So, review your body language and posture if you aren't receiving the response you want.

Your dog may sit in training class or at home, but what about at the beach or at the park with a band playing and children squealing? Desensitize by integrating these events into your dog's life. You can skip, sing, twirl, dance, do aerobic exercises, stretch, and yawn to incite a relaxation cue. Condition those muscles and training skills. Start with small increments. Increase as your dog becomes less moved by your antics (i.e., sits or stays in place). Always reinforce the behavior you want sooner rather than later. Timing is absolutely crucial for shaping behaviors. Snapshot the highlights of acceptable behavior with a praise and reward. And reward with the jackpot for the finest behaviors. This will create the difference between a mediocre response from your dog and a great response.

SIT-STAY AND DOWN-STAY

This is the same as previous weeks, but with the added zest and distance. By now your dog should be used to and responding to both hand and voice signals. You are using variable reinforcement schedules, treating at intervals for the desired sequence of behaviors. Practice your sit-stays and down-stays increasing the distance from your dog (three times, 6 to 10 feet and so forth). Give the stay request. Continue to increase the length of time you maintain (hold) a sit-stay or down-stay (one, two, three minutes). Return to the right around the back of your dog. Pause 5 to 6 seconds. Praise and reward.

Gary and Casidy demonstrate a down-stay. (Photo by Maureen Ross)

STAND

Have your dog stand by using hand or voice signal. Don't forget to say, "stay." Otherwise, if your dog moves from the stand position, it's fine because you didn't request a stay. Lightly run your hands down your dog's back. Avoid petting, as this is a distraction. Your dog must remain in a stand position for one minute. Praise and reward.

TEACH A FAVORITE TRICK

Pick a safe trick: bang-on-your-side, high-five, twirl, back-up, take-a-bow. Tricks are great if they are used and not abused. A trick is something for amusement. It's also helpful. Take bang-on-your-side, for instance. This is great at the vet's office for an exam, or for grooming. The key is to not abuse the trick, for example by making too many requests at one time. A dog shouldn't have to offer tricks to anyone more than a couple of times. Otherwise, the behavior will wear itself out, and it's not fair for the dog.

Casidy enjoys her favorite trick: Bang, roll over! (Photo by Maureen Ross)

RECALL

Continue as in Week #3. Remember to have the dog do a sit-front (i.e., sit in front of you) when she returns to you.

WAIT

With your dog in a sit, tell her to "wait." When you're ready, say, "OK," or "Come on." This is a good behavior to teach for going through doors, getting into cars, or going downstairs. It ensures safety for yourself, for children, and when around older adults. You can also teach your dog to go ahead, forward, and back up.

OFF AND SIT

"Off" is an effective and useful request to manage jumping or to keep dogs off furniture. Begin early; prevent the preventable. The most effective way to eliminate or modify a behavior is to teach what to do and what not to do. A sitting dog cannot jump. It's physically impossible.

HOMEWORK

You should set aside at least 10 minutes, twice a day, for formal training, with as many informal training sessions as possible integrated into everyday living and learning. Practice each of the following:

1. Heel or walk-on-a-loose-leash. Every day.

2. Sit-stays and down-stays for 3 minutes; two times daily. Thirty minutes, three times a week.

3. Add distance and distractions.

4. Recall; five times daily. Add on a sit-front.

5. Add music while training.

Chapter Ten

Lesson Plan: Week #5

HEEL AND WALK-ON-A-LOOSE-LEASH

Continue practicing. This is Week #5, so what more can we say? If you have been diligently following this program, then by this week you should be developing a good understanding and awareness of your relationship with your dog. Walk in different locations with your dog, go longer distances, and add distractions. If you're running into glitches that seem overwhelming, such as constant leash pulling, then seek help from a professional. Be proactive, rather than reactive. Visualize what might happen on a walk before you go on one. Reflect, but do not dwell, on past experiences. What previous behaviors were undesirable to you? What can you do to change this? How would you handle the situation differently? Use a problem-solving chart to jot down the issues and solutions, keeping in mind that you and your dog are in a process of learning and growing together to develop a respectable relationship.

SIT-STAY, PART ONE

We know that this can be boring and tedious. Look at it this way: You are accomplishing something here. You are making a difference. If you are doing a good enough job, you will create a great dog. Chin up, turn, and face your dog. Remember to get your dog's attention first; say, "Watch me." Eye-to-eye communication is magic. Maintain a sit-stay for one minute. Return around the dog to complete the exercise, making the circles around the back of your dog a little bigger each time. Pause five to six seconds (the dog must remain sitting). Praise and reward.

Maureen rewards her friend after a successful sit-stay.
(Photo by Gary Ross)

SIT-STAY, PART TWO

Same as above, but with distractions (twirl, skip, and sing). Praise and reward.

DOWN-STAY

Identical to sit-stay, but in the down position. Maintain for three minutes. Return around the back of the dog, making bigger circles and perhaps slowing your pace so it takes a bit longer to get around. Does your dog maintain the stay? Praise and reward. The dog didn't maintain the stay? Try again and reinforce ... but never give up. Try some down-stays with distractions. Have a friend walk by being joyful or carrying a toy.

Your dog should look to you for cues and remain sitting or in a down-stay until you release him.

STAND

Place your dog in a stand position using hand and/or voice cues. Give the stay request. Pivot in front of your dog. Walk to the end of the lead (six feet). Have someone run their hands down your dog's back (feels good, huh?). After one minute or so, pivot back to your dog, to the right.

Praise and reward.

RECALL

Use your Flexi lead. If you are in a fenced, safe area, try this off-lead, but beware: If your dog turns and runs away just once, you have set a training precedent. She will enjoy the freedom. We guarantee it. Place your dog in a sit-stay. Walk about 10 feet away. Turn and face your dog. Remain standing confidently and proudly. Maintain eye contact. Observe and quiet your mind. Enthusiastically call your dog. When your dog arrives, she will sit-front. Reward with the jackpot if the recall was enthusiastic. So-so response? Praise anyway for coming to you. Didn't come to you? Ran away? Tough luck, no play or treat. Take away the reward (you), and try again later. Go get your dog, be firm, and let her know this isn't satisfactory behavior. A scowling face will do. If your dog comes to you, remember—no punishing.

HOMEWORK

Create a theme for this week's training lesson. We use stovepipe hats. Any different hat will do. Be creative. Make or wear your favorite hat. Train with these hats on. You are desensitizing your dog to different sights, sounds, smells, cultures, and hats. Train as usual.

You should set aside at least 10 minutes, twice a day, for formal training, with as many informal training sessions as possible integrated into everyday living and learning. Practice each of the following:

1. Listen up! Practice *everything*.

2. Walk calmly on loose leash.

3. One-minute sit-stay.

4. Three-minute down-stay.

5. Come-on-recalls.

6. Try out a favorite, safe trick like twirl (the dog twirls, then you twirl).

7. Add some music and play games.

8. Praise, hugs, play. It's therapeutic for you and your dog.

✦ ✦ ✦

Training should be fun, fair, flexible, and forgiving.
Sounds like a good relationship for any species.

✦ ✦ ✦

Chapter Eleven

Lesson Plan: Week #6

Congratulations, you are in Week #6 of the relationship-training program. How do you feel? If you have been experiencing a human power outage or have blended feelings (physical and emotional), this is perfectly normal. Learning for humans can be overwhelming at times, so imagine what it's like for your dog. Don't give up; life is a journey and learning is part of a process.

BUILD THE RELATIONSHIP

Now that you have laid the foundation, it's time to build the house. Then, you may decide to renovate or make additions. The key to short- or long-term joyful success is in the process of doing it in the here and now. Continue the process of building the relationship. How? Learn something new every day.

Relax a bit in the relationship. Take some time every day for personal renewal. Enjoy nature and your dog for no specific reason. We guarantee that when you make up your mind to do something that involves changing patterns that you are familiar with, it will seem difficult at first but it will get easier and easier with practice. It will become an integral and natural part of your lifestyle, and you'll just feel good about doing it.

Be mindful that, like humans, many dogs go through phases when they seem to forget everything they have learned, or lose interest in it. Don't worry. It's not amnesia. It's back to the same old axiom we've used throughout this book: There are many more interesting sights, sounds, and smells to explore, especially when you have a house dog. The environment outside of the house is pure entertainment. Recapture the dog's attention. Identify this clear message from your dog that it's time for a change. Think win-win; then think synergy (1 + 1 = 3). Synergy is simply taking the win-win to a higher level. It's being creative enough to go beyond what you already know, opening your mind to new, but realistic, possibilities. Go the extra distance and take the higher road.

CONTINUE TO TEACH

Occasionally a dog will reach a plateau with a particular behavior you have taught. This is an intricate part of the learning process. It indicates a need for assessment. Teach a new behavior, or teach a same behavior in a different way. Ask for a "sit" while standing with your back to your dog. Ask for a recall and throw a treat or chew toy through your legs. Ferret out boredom with new training techniques and games. As Turid Rugaas says, "Simply taking your dog for a sniff down a different road is mentally stimulating."

Remember that a chain of behaviors is only as strong as its weakest link. When a link becomes too weak, the chain of behaviors falls apart. If your dog sits, but won't stay, then it's no longer relevant to the dog. The response is contingent upon the consequences. If it isn't meaningful to you, it won't be to the dog either. Dogs are clever. The same holds true for incidents that are unbecoming.

Imagine that you're out on a seemingly pleasant walk with your dog and another dog bolts into your dog's face. What a traumatic experience! You were surprised, maybe you screamed. Your dog was startled, and the response may have been to growl or deck the other dog. Maybe your dog was decked. Okay, this can happen. The follow-up—your reaction—will be the deciding factor on how this affects both of you in the future. If this is so traumatic to you that you can't let it go, then your dog will never let it go either. So, take a deep breath, learn from the experience, release, relax, and let it go so you both can grow.

Dogs like it safe not dangerous, pleasurable not painful, and they instinctively know when you don't care. They pick up on every nuance of your emotions and body language. They need to know what their position is in the pack, human or otherwise. "If I do this, this will happen. If I do that, that will happen. What's in it for me?" Remember your ABC's: Antecedent + Behavior = Consequence. For example, you went for the walk and you had a negative incident; you remained as calm as possible while saying something like, "Oh well, what was that, a big silly dog. Come on, let's go the other way." Let it go. What you focus your thoughts on gives them power. Be selective of what you focus on.

HOMEWORK

By this point in the program, you should have integrated many of these (and other) behaviors into your everyday life. For homework, concentrate on those things you're having difficulties with (remember to regress if you need to).

You should set aside at least 10 minutes, twice a day, for formal, focused training, with as many informal training sessions as possible integrated into everyday living and learning. Practice each of the following:

1. Relax, breathe, discover your spirit and savor your dog's spirit (for the rest of your life).

2. Calmly walk-on-a-loose-leash (easy, normal, with attitude).

3. A three-minute sit-stay (increase the distance, change the location).

4. A three-minute down-stay (increase the distance, change the location, add variety).

5. Enthusiastic, joyful come-on-recalls.

6. Integrate the wait with take-its and leave-its often.

7. Maximize the bang for the buck by keeping it fun and pleasurable.

8. Focus energy on the good stuff and provide no free lunch.

9. Be your dog's best friend.

10. Welcome your dog's efforts.

11. Be fair, fun, flexible, and forgiving.

12. Be generous with your praise whenever your dog comes to you.

Section Three

Relationship-Training
Applications

In this section, we'll take the theory that you learned in Section One and the basic training exercises that you learned in Section Two, and apply it to everyday situations. This is the meat and potatoes of relationship training.

Read the following chapters to hone up on your practical skills. If behaviors are perceived as problems, this is where you want to be. If you are having puppy problems, check out Chapter Twelve, "Housetraining." You'll want to acclimate your dog to people, other dogs, and other animals, so follow the suggestions in Chapter Thirteen, "Socialization." Are you having a problem with barking, chewing, digging, or jumping? Check out Chapter Fourteen, "Chewing, Barking, Digging, and Separation Anxiety" for solutions.

Be creative and use this information to develop your own plan of solutions or alternatives. But please, do have a plan and be able to settle for alternatives once in awhile. That way if it doesn't work you can change it or have a backup plan.

We conclude Section Three with Chapter Fifteen, "Using Creative Games to Train," which provides suggestions for training games, and Chapter Sixteen, "Clicker Training," which explores a fun and effective way to train your dog. Sometimes, as we go through our daily routine, we get into a rut or a comfort zone. Ditto with our dogs and training, so spruce it up. Play some games. Go for a walk. Use a clicker device. Make it different and make a difference. Both you and your dog will be better off for it. Plus, your training will be more effective.

Okay, let's do it. Explore your issues and develop unique, creative solutions expressly for you and your dog.

Chapter Twelve

Housetraining

"Housetraining the puppy" ... what a wonderful phrase. It used to be called "housebreaking," and sometimes still is. This never made any sense to us, as this implies that one is going to break something. What? The house, the dog, the dog's spirit by smooshing his nose in it? Housetraining is a process that requires understanding the problem— that the puppy is urinating in the wrong place at the right time, or the pup was in the right place at the wrong time. For example: The puppy was left loose for a lengthy period of time (more than 20 minutes) in the house, and then she eliminated in the living room. The children were supposed to be watching the puppy, or perhaps you thought that at six months, she should be able to hold her bladder all day. Oops ... ever so wrong.

Listen up: Puppies cannot control their bladder for long periods of time until they are at least six months old. This may vary from breed to breed and from situation to situation. A puppy will need to urinate every 20 to 30 minutes or immediately after eating, excited playing, and awakening. They require confinement—in crates, for example—to prevent the problem of eliminating in undesirable places. Confinement for short periods of time will teach control. Most pups won't soil their own den, but if left for unreasonable amounts of time, what choice do they have?

They must be taught, in a positive way, to go outside, then praised every time they do. If you don't catch them in the act, push your pause button, take a deep breath, and let it go. It's absolutely senseless and abusive to traumatize a pup, even five seconds after the act, with reprimands. The act is over and done; the pup is relieved. The old standby of rubbing his nose in it has been put in the dumpster. It doesn't work, never did, and never will. Puppies, or older dogs, know exactly what their own excrement smells like. Showing them that they relieved themselves is counterproductive in training them to eliminate outside and especially in your presence. Why? Because going to the toilet in your presence brings about nasty ramifications.

For humans, problems associated with housetraining puppies are simply about understanding the process of elimination. You cannot cork the volcano, but you can predict with a fair amount of certainty and ingenuity when and where. They usually go back to their same spots if you haven't neutralized the area well with a good cleaner.

Pups have to eliminate, so let's get back to basics for a moment. Understand the process and shape the behavior that you want. Sorry, you cannot decide when puppies have to eliminate, but you can recognize the time and indicative behaviors.

✦ ✦ ✦

"Solve the problem by understanding the process."
—Dr. Ian Dunbar

✦ ✦ ✦

Refer to the "Housetraining at a Glance" sidebar for an easy-to-follow summary of when pups have to go. Read "Myths, Facts, Delusions, and Miracles" and this will set you on the right puppy track. It's fairly clear-cut, but can get muddled in the confusion of excitement, especially in a household with children. In a very sweet and simple nutshell, housetraining requires some consistency and follow-up. Both short-term and long-term confinement will produce different results. Short-term confinement, where you will whisk your puppy outside on a regular basis (every hour at least) to eliminate, then praise profusely, will teach the concept of housetraining. Long-term confinement will require some sort of bathroom area. Whether you use newspaper or pads doesn't matter, but the area should be enclosed so the pup does not have access to the rest of the house. Prevention from making mistakes is a far more pleasant way to learn about where to void, spatially, than waiting for a mistake, followed by some sort of punishment.

Puppies cannot control their bladder for long periods of time until they
are at least six months old. Housetraining requires that you teach a puppy
(or dog) to go outside and praise him every time he does!
(Photo by Winter-Churchill Photography)

Consistent scheduling and supervision of children and playtime are vital elements to optimum housetraining. Feed your pup on a regular schedule and remove the water after a certain time at night. If you are concerned about hydration, leave a couple of ice cubes in the pup's dish. Ensure the pup goes out and eliminates before bedtime. Praise. Stay out a minute or so with the pup. Otherwise, you will teach the pup to delay elimination simply because he wants to have a good sniff.

CRATE HAVEN

A crate is a valuable training tool. Its purpose is to provide security, safety, and protection for short-term confinement while educating a puppy or new dog about house boundaries. When enhanced with doggie accessories—such as Kongs, crate pad, and a clip-on water dish—the crate becomes a cozy haven.

Housetraining at a Glance

Use this quick reference to help your puppy use natural instincts for gentle, quick, and effective housetraining. Post it on your cupboard or refrigerator door.

To prevent undesirable elimination:

- Do not let your puppy wander all over without supervision. Keep the pup confined in a small area like a kennel, crate, or utility room. A baby gate works great. Prevent mistakes and reward desired behaviors.
- When the puppy sniffs and circles around, take her to a desired elimination area. Pups instinctively desire to eliminate after being confined, eating, drinking, playing, resting, or sleeping.
- Feed your puppy a measured amount of food. When the puppy walks away, or after about 10 to 15 minutes, remove the bowl. Then follow the steps below.

Five to 30 minutes after eating, drinking, playing, resting, sleeping, or being confined, follow these steps to help your puppy eliminate in the chosen area:

- Take puppy to the selected place for elimination.
- Say special words that you want your pup to associate with desired behavior.
- When puppy begins to eliminate, say quiet words of praise. Praise again when she's finished. Play for a minute or so. These are life rewards.
- When puppy is done, praise enthusiastically, pet, and reward with food or play.
- Reward each and every time with praise, but as your puppy learns, give food rewards intermittently. Use play or a walk as a motivator for desirable behaviors.

Many people think of a crate as a jail cell, but a dog's perception is much different. Dogs are den animals by nature and will view their crate as a den. Be sure to place the crate so your dog can see the environment and family members. He needs to be able to take in the sights, sounds, and smells of your home to feel like part of the family.

The crate helps you regulate your puppy's schedules for feeding, elimination, and exercise, and it's great for time-outs. In the bedroom, the obvious benefit is that a crated pup can't make mistakes and soil carpets. Dogs usually avoid soiling their dens, so the crate becomes a helpful educational tool for housetraining. And you'll get a peaceful night's sleep because the pup can see you and won't cry as much.

Crates are not recommended for a dog that must be left alone frequently for extended periods of time. Lengthy solitary confinement is psychologically and emotionally cruel. If you must crate your dog for 8 hours, ensure that she gets plenty of exercise and time to eliminate before and after confinement. When you arrive home, the dog comes first. She should be fed, exercised, and allowed some supervised freedom in the house. Crates should never be used for punishment.

A crate should be large enough to permit your dog to stretch on her side without being cramped. It's wise to anticipate: You don't want a crate that's too big, but it should be big enough to last through growth spurts. The dog should be able to stand without hitting her head and be able turn around.

MYTHS, FACTS, DELUSIONS, AND MIRACLES

Unfortunately, our puppies and many adult dogs do not share our enthusiasm for training, primarily because of the way we train. Their attitude is: "Frankly my dear, I'd rather chase chipmunks."

An understanding of how puppies live from moment to moment will help you to grasp some things about training and behavior. Then, we need to look at reframing some of the delusions and consider whether or not we are waiting for miracles.

MYTH: "My friend told me to rub his nose in it. That's what my mother used to do. If I hit him with a newspaper ... If I show him the mistake and scold him ... He knows what he did wrong. ... He thinks my green carpet is grass. ... She gets mad at me when I leave her alone, so she wees all over the house to get back at me. ... He's testing me." Have you said any of these before? Be honest, we all have.

FACT: People raising puppies make these and similar statements. How come? One reason is because this is how we have been taught from generation to generation. Listen up: We are in a new millennium. Times and the environment have changed. Attitudes about dogs and training have changed, too.

Developmental Stages of Puppies

Let's review some of the developmental stages of puppies, and then explore some of the myths surrounding growing puppies. Most pups are acquired between the ages of 7 weeks and 12 weeks. Depending on the breed you have selected (mixed included), housetraining can take from two days to several weeks depending on training techniques.

A puppy of seven to eight weeks has had someone else to look after the responsibilities of cleaning up. First, it was Mom. The mother dog must induce the puppy to relieve himself from the time of birth by licking the pup's belly and genital area. She did not scold the pup for doing what comes naturally—relieving herself. In fact, she cleaned it up just like humans change a baby's diapers.

Puppies under the age of 12 weeks seldom have the maturity necessary to understand housetraining, let alone self-control or attention span. By 12 weeks, most pups are adjusting to their new environment. They are left with Mother Nature and her urges, plus a bunch of newspapers, which they have no interest in reading, but tearing them up might be fun.

DELUSION: New owners usually select their pup and take him home. With good intentions, they have thought of everything: bed, food, toys, leash, veterinarian. Once they have reached the family room rug, they think of his bathroom habits. Whoops. How flabbergasted new owners are when their pups arrive, greet the children or cat (an exciting new experience), and proceed to christen the carpet. After all of that preliminary planning, too. Within approximately 30 minutes of entering a new home, a pup is facing defacing—"No, no, no, bad puppy!", then with a smack, "Outside!" The pup is listening intently and hearing, "Blah, blah, blah, puppy, blah blah, blah!"—and suddenly, "Ouch, hey, what was *that* for?"

FACT: It was a long way home (at least 15 minutes). The pup is curious and searching for the warmth of his littermates. "Where's Mom?" Then, he notices the kids. "Okay, this is good. They are about my size, so maybe this won't be so bad. Yahoo!" Piddle. "Whoops, back outside!"

DELUSION: Some new owners believe that puppies of this age can hold their bladder endlessly, like a stuffed dog.

FACT: Puppies can go only a matter of minutes between piddles. They also need to be taught where to go and when. Usually after greeting the family with a puddle on the carpet, he receives a reprimand, silence, or some very strange looks. Either way, the lesson is missed.

MYTH: Many novice owners will show the pup his mistake and maybe rub his nose in it. Perhaps they will swat him with the newspaper (the same material you expect him to relieve himself on later). Then, they may whisk him outside. They believe this will teach him what he did wrong.

FACT: At this early point in the ritual of greeting the new puppy, he has already learned how much attention he gets when he leaves you a "gift" on the carpet. Attention is attention regardless of how pleasant or unpleasant. It can be positive attention full of praise and reinforcement for "good" behavior, or it can be negative attention full of reprimands reinforcing "bad" behavior. The pup quickly learns to revel in attention, good or bad. Bestowing attention on the puppy, in these early stages, sends a message of, "Wow, whatever I did, it must have been great! Whenever I piddle on the rug everyone comes running over—I must be wonderful. When I bark or whine in front of company, they pet me, so I'll go for the 'Oscar' next time. When I throw a tantrum, they give me a biscuit."

The cycle begins. Puppies do what comes naturally and get rewarded for it. As Dr. Dunbar shares in his *Good Little Dog Book*, "[T]his is *unintentional training* and very easy to do. If you have rubbed his nose in it, you have taught him that defecating is wrong, and it smells awful. Whose doesn't?"

DELUSION: You actually believe she will go right away.

FACT: She senses that in a few moments you may have a panic attack. She relieves herself in her designated area. "Yes, hurry up, we're going in." You have inadvertently taught your puppy that as soon as she relieves herself, she is quickly escorted inside; no exercise or play, just another boring soliloquy of "good girls." "Are you talking to me? Next time, I'll take my time, so we can stay outside longer, or I'll fake a whiz. Then, I'll go on the carpet. I get more attention that way." Let your puppy know that she is good beyond words for relieving herself quickly in the appropriate place. Take a short walk, play, let her sniff, and throw a few balls before going indoors.

Cleaning Up!

What you did to the puddle after you found it makes all the difference in the world through the eyes of a puppy.

MYTH: "Quick, clean it up with soap and water. ... Ammonia and water is what my grandmother used. ... Sally says to blot it dry with paper towels, then show the puppy the towels. ... I use expensive puppy stain remover. Oh my gosh, the carpet is changing colors. ... Quick, let's air it out." ... And the absolute worst: "Hit her; she'll get the message."

FACT: Most people feel horrible after hitting a defenseless puppy. Dogs have an acute sense of smell. After you have knocked yourself out trying to mask the odor, dogs will return to "their" spot. It's natural for dogs (both genders) to mark "their" territory by urinating. Prevention is the goal. Most of us cannot devote every waking second to watching our puppy. We are human—not perfect or consistent.

MIRACLE! You have already put your puppy in the "land of no mistakes" by confining him to a safe and acceptable area. You are preventing the preventable. Bravo!

If you can catch the tinkler in the act, scoop him up and take him to his designated bathroom area, preferably outside. Don't get trapped into thinking that paper training, although convenient, will eventually teach him not to go in the house. It teaches him to go in the house on papers. Guaranteed, if you have chosen a large or giant-breed dog, you will very soon want this puppy relieving himself outside.

Remain with your pup until he relieves himself, praise him, take a short walk, and toss a stick or ball. Now, go back in the house. Clean up that mistake, but do not do it in front of the pup. You do not want him to see you giving more attention to that mistake than is necessary. Neutralize the spot with a good odor neutralizer (such as Fresh n Clean, Nilodor, Nature's Miracle, or Natra Pet). In a pinch, mix white vinegar in equal strength with water. Spray thoroughly and apply several layers of paper towels. Discard the paper towels. Don't bother showing them to your pup.

MYTH: "She knows better. ... She just does it to get back at me. ... She just went outside, now she comes in the house and goes on the floor. ... I can't take this anymore! ... Boo-hoo, boo-hoo!"

DELUSION: Oh, please! You have been watching too many movies if you really believe that the pup is actually strategizing how he can use elimination as revenge. Be accountable for your emotions and teach the puppy where and when to eliminate.

FACT: Puppies do not know any better. Adopted adult dogs may not have been trained to know any better, either. In fact, they may have been inadvertently trained to be obnoxious. Before jumping to conclusions, give yourself and your dog a break. The message was not communicated effectively.

MIRACLE! It's a miracle to know that puppies learn much quicker than human babies do at this early stage of development. They are extremely adaptable. How long does it take to potty-train a human child? Do we expect them to control themselves before ages that they are capable of doing so?

Children learn and try to please. Puppies do, too, but are expected to do it in a very short time. It's true that their age is compressed relative to a human's. They learn behaviors quickly in spite of the fact that many messages are being communicated to them in different voices. A 1-year-old puppy is equivalent to a 15-year-old teenager. We wouldn't conceive of waiting until a child is 15 years old to begin teaching him the ABC's. Begin informal, positive training early. Teach the puppy what you want the adult dog to know.

URINEDIPPIDITY: Housetraining is an art requiring observation and creativity. As the pup grows, develops, and matures, so do his bladder, bowels, and self-control. He will be able to go for longer stretches between potty times. Train yourself to be observant and watch for signs. Puppies will need to go as soon as they wake up, after they have eaten, and after they have played for 15 to 20 minutes. Think ahead and do not assume that your puppy carries the *Encyclopuppia Britannica on What Humans Expect* in his little head. A pearl of wisdom is to continue planning after the puppy comes home. Expect blips in your original plans and make the necessary modifications. This includes the supervision of children. For example, if you withhold food and water after 7:00 P.M., your puppy will not dehydrate before morning. Scoop him up and outside. By six months old, you will experience urinedippidity. Your pup will be holding his bladder through the night and for many hours during the day.

DELUSION: We bought the pup for the children. It's their job to take care of him.

MANY FACTS: Ha ha. Please read "Children and Dogs" in Chapter Thirteen. If the children allow the puppy to eat, drink, and play freestyle, you, as the parents, will be faced with the enormous challenge of reshaping a repertoire of undesirable behaviors.

The pup will not learn the meaning of "settle-down" if left alone to play unsupervised with children under the age of 12 (unless they are extremely precocious).

DELUSION: Lifestyles today predicate that a dog may be left alone for up to eight hours at a time. This doesn't mean that one should deprive oneself the joy of canine companionship. However, expecting a puppy to spend an entire day, loose in the house, without doing anything is a fantasy. You must have seen *The Wizard of Oz* or read *Harry Potter* too many times. To a puppy, everything is a play toy; pure enjoyment and entertainment.

BE PROACTIVE, NOT REACTIVE: When you arrive home, do you look around at the destruction, smell the bouquet of odors, then flail at the pup, face scrunched up bellowing, "What the heck have you done! No, no, no—bad, bad, *bad* dog!" and maybe even a whack. If you don't, then "good human" to you.

FACT: If you do not catch your little interior decorator in the act, let it go. It may make you feel good to drag her to the spot to point out how completely disgusted you are with her behavior. It will serve little purpose in teaching your pup the whys and why-nots. What you have taught her is that it is extremely unpleasant to greet you at the door.

MIRACLE! The miracle is you have the resources to help you make all of this easier. Prevent the pup from causing destruction by confining him in an area like an indoor/outdoor kennel, crate, exercise pen, or homemade den in the basement. Use baby gates as a barrier to other rooms.

Chapter Thirteen

Socialization

Socialization is a continuing process whereby an individual (or a dog) learns and assimilates the values and behavior patterns to his or her culture and social position. Wow! This speaks volumes when it comes to socialization and dogs. They are thrust from their own culture (littermates and Mom) to a human culture. In a sense, what we need to do as humans for our dogs is to help them be "fit for life" in companionship with humans and familiarize them with surroundings that they will encounter on a daily basis.

LOOKING AND LEARNING

Socialization is a precious gift that we give our dogs and should be tops on the agenda for all puppies. Good breeders will carefully socialize puppies from the time they are born. The more sights, sounds, smells, environments and cultures that your pup has been exposed to, preferably in a positive way, the better adjusted and confident he will be as an adult dog. Even negative encounters will teach a lesson if they are counteracted and followed up with a positive response from you, as a respected pack leader. Your reaction to day-to-day living experiences will grow on your dog. For example, do you get overly emotional around your dog when you go for a walk and another dog appears? This other dog may be a menace, but if you're proactive (see the other dog coming in advance and act appropriately by going the other way, or grounding your dog with a sit) then the situation will not be a negative life-altering experience for either of you.

There is no "guessing" here. This works. Even if your dog is a couch potato who only goes out once a week to the post office with you, the more that he has been introduced gently to children, other dogs, cars, cows, ducks, and geese, the more likely that this walk to the post office will be a joyful one rather than one fraught with overexuberance or fear.

We have been asked many times how to "train my dog to be neutral around dogs and children." The standard answer is, "The only truly neutral dog in this world is either stuffed or dead." It doesn't exist, in our opinion. Every dog, child, or situation that your dog interacts with will present a different set of circumstances. It's ludicrous to think that anyone can pinpoint exactly what "triggers" a dog to chase a rabbit when he hasn't in the past. Chances are the answer here is he has the predator instinct that most dogs have.

Our advice is to not dwell on "why" the dog did what she did; just begin from that point on with what you would like her to do in a similar situation and shape that behavior to a controllable level. If this behavior has occurred once, chances are it will again in related circumstances. Therefore, be aware. Anticipate what may happen. Visualize how you will redirect your dog's focus to you in a positive manner. The "Positive Problem Solving" exercise in Chapter Fourteen will be helpful.

TOTALLY TOLERANT?

In class, we have met some lovable breeds with reputations of being antisocial. Standoffish sometimes, stressed and anxious maybe, but a well-socialized dog will tolerate children, people, and other dogs under the watchful guidance of its human. It's true that some individual dogs and breeds may require more socializing than others, but it's the human's responsibility to be cognizant of this and take responsibility for doing it.

The way you socialize your dogs with children, other dogs, and different species is essential to achieve a positive outcome on a more regular basis. You may not reach a 100 percent success rate, but with a little bit of socializing effort, you can raise those odds to a comfortable and manageable level. The information in this chapter will help prepare your dog for life in the real world. Integrating a few things each day into your lifestyle will create a well-adjusted companion that you can rely on with hopefulness in almost any situation.

CHILDREN AND DOGS

Children and dogs go together like strawberries and whipped cream. In small portions, eaten slowly and savored, it's a delicacy. In large portions, eaten quickly, it will make you sick.

Social Relationships

Learning to respect, care for, and participate in training a puppy can give an enormous boost to a child's self-esteem. It's vital that the dog's transition from puppy through adolescence into adulthood be successful, so that both the child and dog can develop confidence in the relationship and their abilities.

Children need supervision around puppies, pure and simple. Leaving them alone together can be catastrophic. Parents and children need to be realistic. Real-world dogs need real-world training. Families need to be involved in the process together. Parents have full responsibility for a pup with the understanding that children will participate in feeding schedules, exercise, and timed-supervised play. The regimen for child-training-dog is one behavior at a time, gently and supervised.

Picture this all too familiar scenario. Puppies and children play. During play, puppies nip, tear, jump, and bark. Children squeal and wiggle their spaghetti-like arms through the air. This incites more nipping, tearing, jumping, and barking. The puppy becomes an adolescent dog (developmentally, a one-year-old pup is equal to a 15-year-old teenager). The adolescent dog strongly objects to this manhandling. He gives a warning by backing off, or giving a little growl. (Refer to Chapter Three, "Recognizing Canine Calming Signals," and "Growling" in Chapter Two) Eventually, the child gets hurt. The dog gets reprimanded (or worse), for doing exactly what she was taught to do—play rough, bark, and jump.

Unfortunately, in these cases, having a dog is perceived as not "working out" for some families. If not handled carefully, the lesson for the children could be that relationships are temporary and dogs are disposable. The child's self-esteem is deflated, along with the dog's spirit and formative first year. Then the adolescent dog is placed in a shelter or another home. He brings along the behavior he has learned, which likely won't work out any differently with another family with children. So, it's an insidious scenario that, unfortunately, ends with many beautiful dogs, who have the potential for being lovely companions, being first misunderstood, abused, and then euthanized.

Learning to respect, care for, and participate in training a dog
can be a wonderful experience for a child.
(Photo by Maureen Ross)

To coexist amicably, children need to be taught respect for dogs, other species, nature, and people. The solution: Socialize, supervise, and teach the children how to act around dogs.

✦ ✦ ✦

Encourage hug-o-war rather than tug-o-war games with children ... and supervise training!

✦ ✦ ✦

Fostering the Relationship

Children under 12 are not perceived as pack leaders by a dog. They're perceived more as playmates. Children are not capable (mentally or physically) of holding onto the leash of a pulling dog. Any correction that a child gives will be meaningless, thus setting them both up for failure. Children need to learn to control the dog by being taught training techniques they can master successfully. Using food treats as lures works exceptionally well with children. For one thing, it puts the pup's focus on the food and not on the fingers. It makes training a pleasurable and easy learning experience.

Strengthen the dog's relationship with family members by being a good role model for the children. Be gentle with the dog. Use positive reinforcement training techniques to shape the desired behavior you would like to see in the adult (pup and child). Use punishment sparingly or not at all.

Teach Your Puppies Well

• Teaching is a more effective, pleasant, and motivating learning tool.
• Teach the pup to enjoy children.
• Teach the children how to enjoy the pup.
• Teach both how to respect each other.
• The lessons will be carried into adulthood for both species.

Children are exemplary at training pups under the guidance of a good mentor. Like puppies, kids are uninhibited and naturally curious. They watch and give things a whirl without prior premeditating, calculating, or strategizing. They aren't as concerned about getting embarrassed. Most of the time, they laugh it off.

GUIDELINES FOR RESPONSIBILITY AND CARE

Here are some basic guidelines to help nurture and develop a healthy relationship between children and dogs:

• Children from infancy to about 5 years of age: Closely supervise interactions between children and dogs. Never leave them alone together.

• Children from 5 to about 14: In this age group, children can assist with dog-care tasks such as feeding, keeping the water dish filled, grooming, yard patrol (clean-ups), visiting the veterinarian, walking, and supervised play sessions (with adults setting the boundaries).

• Children from 14 to about 18: Teenagers can handle most of the responsibility for their dogs. However, be mindful that teens are going through some difficult transitional stages in their own development. They have demands on their time and emotions. Parents need to remain responsible caretakers and coaches. Ensure that the teens don't inadvertently neglect the dog ("I forgot"). A dog left outside in the heat without shade or water could die!

• Teach children how to move slowly and speak softly around dogs (may your higher spirits be with you on achieving this one).

• Teach a calming exercise regularly. The children and the dog sit or lie on the floor quietly for five minutes (or more if age-appropriate), followed by a supervised play session.

• Teenagers should do the previous exercise for 30 minutes a few times a week while watching a good program. Nine- to 12-year-olds should go for about 15 minutes. This exercise will help build trust and affection between the child and dog while teaching both parties how to "settle-down" and take a "time-out."

• Set realistic and achievable expectations that are age- and experience-appropriate for dogs and children.

• Dogs can learn to play other games with children such as retrieve, hide-and-seek, and find-the-biscuit. It gives them an activity that directs their natural instincts and energy in a positive outlet.

OTHER DOGS AND OTHER SPECIES

First things first. The most important thing for you and your dog is that she be well socialized and people-friendly. Socialization is a lifelong process. It has a beginning. It has no end. Once your dog is comfortable around people, turn your attention to socializing her to other dogs and other animals.

Dog with Dogs

Given today's society, is it a necessity that your dog be dog-friendly? No. Is it a nicety? Absolutely. Just take a walk around town. We live in a rural/suburban setting with primarily single-family dwellings on one-plus acre lots. When we take our dogs for a walk in our neighborhood, we generally don't see any other dogs. We hear them, but don't see any out for walks. On the rare occasion that we do, it's usually off-leash, which isn't "walking etiquette" and unsafe for the dogs.

From talking with other folks around the country, this appears to be the rule rather than the exception in suburbia. In urban areas, a different dictum applies. The expanse of multifamily dwellings and the absence of individual yards require walking your dogs for both elimination and exercise. Even in this environment, dog-to-dog interaction can be limited. All activity, at least in theory, is on-leash, unless we visit the dog park, in which case all of our dog's socialization skills come into play.

Like socialization with people, dog-to-dog socialization is a lifelong process. In addition, there are no guarantees that your dog will cozy up to another with a playbow and friendly wag. Many of us do an admirable job starting out. We go to puppy school and seek out lots of interaction with a number of other dogs. We bone up on our housetraining skills. At approximately six months to a year, we stop, assuming that the pup should now instinctively, intellectually, and intuitively know what comes next behaviorally in life. Sound exaggerated? It isn't. Just ask any dog trainer or behaviorist how many calls he or she receives regarding behavioral problems for dogs that are one to two years old. Do some research at the local SPCA. The numbers will shock you. And it's very sad and disheartening to see so many beautiful, potentially delightful canine companions wasted to euthanasia or bounced from one home to another due to misunderstandings about their "natural" behaviors or "conditioned by the owner" negative behaviors.

As mentioned, at one year of age, a dog is developmentally equivalent to a 15-year-old teenager. Would any of us drop the curtain on all boundaries and teaching experiences for a 15-year-old human? Would any of us say, "Okay, you're in high school now, so you're on your own"? Of course not. That would be giving a teenager too many options to choose from, leading them down some dangerous pathways that they could have avoided had they continued receiving mentoring from wiser adults.

Unfortunately, when most dogs hit adolescence, dog-to-dog socialization goes downhill because of this illusion that we have done our "jobs" and that our dogs will get along with anyone. In reality, it can be a shocking wake-up call the first time our dog rolls another dog face-first in the sand.

At a year old, the dog is going into a phase that needs even more positive reinforcing and socializing with dogs and people in different locales. During adolescence and throughout all stages of their lives, dogs must be continually socialized. Their confidence needs to be buoyed, their spirits reassured, and new training techniques introduced to maintain motivation. Unless we are vigilant, problems can develop, even amongst multiple-dog households.

Dogs play. Sometimes they argue. Some dogs are quite content to never see another dog, while others prefer the connection, stimulation, and play. Our personal opinion comes straight from Noah. We believe it's pleasing to have two of any species, so that they know that there is someone like them around. This doesn't necessarily mean that they agree or will get along, but it makes us feel good.

The key, for most of us, is whether or not the dogs have learned how to argue and/or play effectively without receiving or inflicting serious injury. Controlling the play does this. Dogs learn this from other dogs that are savvy at the "game" and have good calming signals.

Humans can teach this by stopping the game every few minutes. Don't allow game playing to escalate into atomic warfare. That's when someone, either of the two-legged variety or the four-legged kind, can get hurt. Gain control by having them do some doggy push-ups. Reward them for taking the time to "pause" and pay attention to you. Then, let them resume playing. This teaches the difference between right and wrong.

Dogs and Cats

Dogs and cats can cohabit quite well if introduced slowly and on their terms, not ours. Be aware that some dogs will always like to chase cats or fast-moving objects. The good news is that most cats run quicker than dogs. If they don't, and you have even the slightest bit of doubt, then don't chance it.

The introduction of any species to another species (and even within the same species) is relatively the same: Use common sense, go slow, and begin on neutral territory. Do your homework before you impulsively bring the cat, bird, hamster, or potbellied pig home. For example, don't assume that your eight-year-old Airedale wants a companion because you think it's a good idea. You might want to ask him first. The reality is that some dogs and cats are quite content to live in a one-animal household.

Use common sense for an appropriate and safe introduction. Ask friends who have done this successfully. If you decide to introduce a kitten into the family, have a baby gate up so the kitten can view the household. Otherwise, keep it confined for periods of time in the bathroom.

Cats have claws and dogs have big teeth. We are not suggesting that you allow the cats and dogs to duke it out because a dog could lose an eye and a cat could get squashed. It shouldn't escalate to this if you have planned carefully and are managing the situation with boundaries and leadership. Do your homework in advance and prepare the environment that they will share. Both dogs and cats should have a hideaway. Cats will find their own.

As with bringing a human baby home from the hospital, try not to change your current companion's routine suddenly. Maintain a consistent schedule and give the same quality attention as your did prior to the new arrival.

We have found that, generally, well-socialized dogs usually accept cats. We say "generally" and "usually" because every circumstance will predicate a different response. Cats will tolerate and very often enjoy brief encounters with a dog. We have three cats and four dogs. They will share a dognapper one minute and chase each other around the next. It can be unpredictable but seldom dangerous. They seem to instinctively respect and tolerate one another's presence and, at times, actually thrive on it. If your dogs have been socialized and introduced prior to bringing home a kitten, your chances of a warm and cozy friendship, or at least respectful living arrangements, will be greater.

Other Dog-Cat Tips

• Litter boxes: Keep litter boxes in an appropriate place so the dogs can't eat cat droppings.
• Private eateries: Allow the cats and dogs to have private dining areas; it's healthier and safer.
• Cat tree houses are great. Most cats will find a high perch to view the scenery and use as a launching pad.

Characteristics of a Healthy Relationship

How many of the following attitudes and behaviors are present in your relationships?

❑ Communication is open and spontaneous (including listening).
❑ Rules and boundaries are clear and explicit, yet allow for flexibility.
❑ Individuality, freedom, and personal identity are enhanced.
❑ Each enjoys doing things for self as well as for the other.
❑ Play, humor, and having fun together is commonplace.
❑ Each does not attempt to "fix" or "control" the other.
❑ Acceptance of self and other (for our real selves).
❑ Assertiveness: feelings and needs are expressed.
❑ Humility: ability to "let go" of need to "be right."
❑ Self-confidence and security in one's own worth.
❑ Conflict is faced directly and resolved.
❑ Openness to constructive feedback.
❑ Each is trustful of the other.
❑ Balance of giving and receiving.
❑ Negotiations are fair and democratic.
❑ Tolerance: forgiveness of self and of others.
❑ Mistakes are accepted and learned from.
❑ Willingness to take risks and be vulnerable.
❑ Other meaningful relationships and interests exist.

❑ Each can enjoy being alone, and privacy is respected.
❑ Personal growth, change, and exploration is encouraged.
❑ Continuity and consistency are present in the commitment.
❑ Balance of oneness (closeness) and separation from each other.
❑ Responsibility for own behaviors and happiness
(not blaming others).

✦ ✦ ✦

Developing healthy relationships is an important life skill that is transferable to work, family, career, and joyful living!

✦ ✦ ✦

Chapter Fourteen

Chewing, Barking, Digging, and Separation Anxiety

It's time to give yourself some praise. You're doing an outstanding job if you've made it to this point in the book—bravo! Now, we'll talk you through some of the toughest areas for new puppy owners, the family dog, and even some of us more experienced trainers.

Issues inevitably come up about managing the natural behaviors of dogs, such as chewing, digging, barking, and jumping. Some of the most teeth-wrenching, hair-pulling, blood vessel-popping experiences can be avoided or redirected into a positive energy-producing outlet for your pup.

Chewing, digging, barking, jumping, and even rolling in what the dog perceives as cologne (smelly stuff like dead fish, horse manure, etc.) are all doggie things to do. Some breeds are predisposed to some of these behaviors. Remember that we made them that way. Terriers like to dig. Herding dogs will bark and gather. Cutting off one of these behaviors will result in an increase in some of the other behaviors. The energy has to come out somewhere. Give them a job to do. Teach them when to bark, where to dig, whom to herd, what to retrieve, and when to protect. Teach them the difference and you will both be at an advantage.

CHEWING

A chew toy is a nondestructible, nonconsumable item that gainfully employs your dog in a gratifying and rewarding occupation. It prevents the dog from chewing "unmentionables" and "unacceptables."

✦ ✦ ✦

Chew toys should not be articles of clothing that you do not want your dog to chew later on: shoes, slippers, sneakers, underwear, old socks, and so on.

✦ ✦ ✦

What Kind of Chew Toys?

There are a number of quality chew toys on the market. Chew toys should be made of hard rubber or, in the case of Activity Balls and Buster Cubes, very hard plastic. Kongs, sterilized cow bones, TennisBones are excellent. Hard rubber balls, big enough so that a St. Bernard cannot swallow it during a catch, are great.

Be a wise shopper. Choose quality, long-lasting, and safe toys. As mentioned previously, quality toys may cost more, but they are safer and last longer. However, a dog will get a lot of mileage out of sweatshirt arms tied in knots. Local fabric stores run sales all the time. Pick up yards of fake lambskin, cut them into strips, braid them, and tie them into knots—voilà ... chew toys!

Rawhide, and pig and cow ears and feet, should be sterilized and doled out only in moderation, in our opinion. Remember that rawhide is a food source of undeterminable ingredients. Rawhide is not a good substitute as a nutritional food source or for a voracious chewer. It can be torn into large strips and swallowed and become lodged in the dog's digestive tract.

Latex and vinyl are not recommended. Most dogs will tear and devour them in a matter of nanoseconds. It's not cost effective, but more importantly, it can be a health hazard if ingested.

Chew Therapy and Shaping the Behavior

Chewing is a natural and basic instinct for dogs. Dogs chew out of necessity and develop chewing habits. Puppies chew to massage their gums while teething. Chewing helps to maintain healthy jaws and teeth. Mature dogs chew to alleviate loneliness and boredom, to relieve anxiety, and for pure enjoyment.

The Toy Box!

We recommend a toy box for your dog. Buy a child's toy box, or be creative and make one. Either way, it can be a central discovery and storage zone for your dog's toys. Teach her to pick out one or two toys for her day's recreation, and to put them back at the end of the day.

It's not necessary to give your dog more than a few toys at a time. Doing so may cause overstimulation or boredom. Begin slowly to teach your puppy what to chew and where to chew. Make this an exhilarating challenge for the pup.

Introduce your puppy to chew toys at the same time that you introduce him to his crate or safe "time-out" area. Make it a positive experience that will inspire confidence in the pup.

Throw in a few healthy, safe chew toys to amuse her. Touch the toys so they hold your scent. This will relax the pup when you need to leave the house. Upon arrival home, release the pup from the crate for greetings and elimination, then excitedly ask her to "find the chew toy" for you, like it is going to save your life. Make chew toys a highlight. Spotlight and shape the behavior that you desire.

After getting your dog eager about her chew toys, observe. Snapshot the moment that she spontaneously picks up her chew toy on her own, rather than an unmentionable. Praise and reward pronto. If she confiscates an unacceptable item, try saying "leave-it" and "sit." Instantaneously give her the appropriate item to chew. This is "chew therapy" in a nutshell. It's effective, time-efficient, and pleasurable.

The Art of Stuffing

Stuffing chew toys increases the intrinsic value of them to the dog. It's like getting a bonus CD with a new computer game.

Stuff your Kongs and cow bones with kibble, biscuits, and other creative menu items (healthy liver treats, low-fat turkey dogs, cheese). Dab a tiny bit of cheese spread or low-fat peanut butter on the ends, enticing the dog to explore into the crevices of that cow-bone cave. Think outside of the box to create your own ideas, while considering caloric intake and health.

BARKING

Why Do Dogs Bark?

Dogs bark (or vocalize) to communicate a message. They bark for a variety of other reasons: to greet, to alert, out of boredom, to get attention, or for the sheer enjoyment of expressing themselves.

Barking is kindred to a human talking. As humans, we can express ourselves in a variety of different ways with our voice: we laugh, whisper, hum, talk, cry, shout, babble, nag, sing, and whistle.

Communication Is a Two-Way Connection

When humans communicate, they usually expect some kind of response. Barking dogs do, too. If they don't get it, they will bark even more. With this, most dogs are met with a reprimand or forced somehow to stop barking. This is counterproductive and abusive.

Metaphorically, it would be like a human having a strong piece of duct tape put over his mouth and then being placed in a dark room for a few days. If you couldn't speak, how would you communicate your emotions, wants, needs, desires, and frustrations? How would you engage someone in conversation, activities, or play? How would you develop your social skills? Perhaps you would improvise by miming, jumping, drawing, and making frantic bodily gestures. One way or another, we all need some sort of interaction with another living being or risk suffering severe deprivation and possibly insanity.

Shape the Barking

We have established that dogs already know how to eat, sit, stand, lie down, jump, paw, lick, play, and roll over. They are extraordinarily adept at developing survival and defense mechanisms to cope. They know instinctively how to bark, whine, or yodel. As human companions, we are not teaching them how to do what comes naturally. We are shaping when, where, and how we expect them to do it, in a savvy man-ner, among the human population.

As with any other behavior, barking can be put on cue for most dogs. Dogs are social animals. Barking usually occurs when they are left in a position that incites them to bark: alone on a cable run; loose in the yard; chained to a dog house; confined in a basement, kennel, or crate for an interminable length of time; or out on a walk in different loca-tions that they have never been assertively, and positively, introduced to before.

These imposed situations create a monotonous barking dog. It becomes a losing battle between owner and dog, and barking becomes an insidious habit. A dog left on a cable run, where they can view but not interact freely with children and other dogs playing, will create a barking dog. Children romping back and forth alongside the dog (on or off of a cable run) will create a jumping, barking dog. The dog is in essence set up for failure when he is allowed into the home to see if he can behave. The outcome is a jumping, barking dog in the home; exactly the way they were taught outside. Who is responsible? Pick up a mirror—you are.

Put Barking on Cue

Pretend you are the maestro of a symphony orchestra. Remember that dogs have to bark, so eliminating barking isn't the objective here. The goal is to orchestrate where, how long, at whom, and when you want your dog to perform the barking symphony. As with any behavior shap-ing, focus on rewarding the behavior you desire *tout de suite*. When your dog doesn't bark for as few as three seconds, quickly praise and reward. Timing is imperative. If you wait, you have forfeited the opportunity to capture a "magical" moment in directing the barking concerto.

Begin by snapshooting silences. Seriously, if your dog is quiet and barking is an issue for you with your dog, then praise the "quiet." Thus, you are shaping "quiet." Cease any tactile contact with your dog, like petting, when your dog barks. Touching exacerbates barking. Contrary to popular belief, this does not calm a habitually barking dog. When you caress a dog while barking, essentially, you are giving carte blanche approval to "please bark some more because I'll caress you." It's contra-dictory to your goal and a confusing message to the dog.

Though petting your dog has therapeutic benefits and lowers blood pressure, it's not healthy for the dog if you pet excessively or unneces-sarily. Most dogs do not want or need to be catered to constantly. This is a behavior that is created by the "human." It makes us feel good, but it's not always that way for the dog.

Get motivated. Consider shaping barking as a challenge. The game is to strategize what, when, where, and how long you want your dog to bark. Be flexible because this will never be perfect. It will be a perfect "whatever it is." Dogs will inevitably bark at chipmunks, squirrels, and other stimuli in new environments. Integrate this into your lifestyle with the dog through socialization. It takes courage to change and practice to get it right.

CUING DIFFERENT VOLUMES

Choose your words carefully. For example, our Newf, Sage, is an energetic barker. She loves to hear her bark echo through the woods and so do we, so we inadvertently shaped the behavior by smiling and giggling every time she does it. We knew this from the get-go, so Sage was taught to express herself at different octaves for the sake of nature and the neighbors. We prompt her with "whisper," "shout," "shush," "listen," and "watch." When we say "shush," "watch," and "Listen, what's that?," Sage responds as if to say, "I don't know, but maybe we should check it out." She relishes this as an opportunity to go exploring. She has a job to do now. The follow-through is for her to find something: "oh look, it was 'Chewman' or 'Stuffy' hiding behind the tree!" Sage still likes to hear herself bark, but by putting this on cue with games, she has a constructive outlet for vocalizing in harmony with nature.

For "whisper," use a subtle movement by clicking together your index finger and thumb. The movement, or cue, and voice request does not have to be elaborate. Sometimes less is better, so keep it simple. For "speak" or "shout," open and close your hand (like a talking puppet).

"Listen" is more difficult but oodles of fun. Looking very expressive, put your hand to your ear and say, "listen." If you receive a quiet, positive response of course, praise and reward. Your intonation and facial expression speaks volumes to the dog. Change them to fit the request and change the dog's mind. Channel the barking into a positive outlet.

You can put "shush" on cue *while your dog is barking*, when you are convinced that you have practiced enough so that the dog understands the difference between barking and not barking. For example: If your dog begins barking, walk over and say "shush" or "quiet." If your dog stops barking for one second, praise, or click if you are clicker training. The timing has to be lickety-split, and using a clicker will enhance timing because they are quick. The association must be positive. Let them know that this is exactly what you expect ... "yes" or "bravo!"

To get dogs to stop barking if they don't stop on their own is more complicated. Humans generally get into a "barking chorus" with their dog. You yell, and they bark louder. The dog is thrilled that you are joining in to serenade the neighborhood. The neighbors may have a different viewpoint.

Sit with your dog, his dinner dish, and kibble. Shape barking for five minutes every day. Add in a few sits and downs. Make him work for his meal. Always end on an achievement, however small.

Redirect the barking. "Listen," "watch," or "What's that?" are excellent ways to do this. Modify the dog's behavior without setting yourself up to become a "barking butler"; for example, when the dog barks, don't just pet him and throw a ball. Instead, wait until you hear silence. At that moment, just throw the ball. Later on, add a "shush" at an opportune time so that you make the connection between quiet, or shush, and bark.

Once you put barking on cue, you have developed a respectful way of controlling the barking to a certain degree. Create your own unique cue of communication with your dog that no one else will be able to botch. Dogs easily become adept at responding to hand and voice cues. This can be handy in a public place.

DIGGING

In the wild, wolves dig dens for their pups. Domesticated dogs dig to bury bones, make dens and cooling holes, relieve stress, or just for the sheer joy of it. They like to nuzzle into a "special spot" to sleep, kick back, and take in the vistas and aromas of a delightful day. Dogs that are confined for extended periods of time dig to escape from the Alcatraz of boredom.

Dogs are archeologists by nature, searching for fossils and bones. They dig with a zesty gusto, using their exquisitely keen senses to forage out scents. How discouraging it can be if every time they attempt their "dig," they are reprimanded for making holes in the lawn. The indignity of it all. These are more than mere holes to the dog.

The "Ignore" Score

One of the easiest ways to cease an annoying behavior, whether barking, jumping, chewing, or mouthing, is to ignore it. Turn around and present your "back" to your dog. If necessary, walk away and hide yourself for a couple of minutes. Zoom back the second your dog stops barking. If you can't run, have a friend hide behind a tree and reward for every "silence." Though you have the capability to do this on your own, teamwork is helpful; it speeds behavior shaping or modification, and gives you support. It's very difficult to be constantly switched on and tuned in to what you are doing with your dog. So, having a cohort is a perk. It also gives you someone to process with afterward, receiving valuable feedback. This can be a grateful tension reliever.

How would anyone of us like it if every time we gregariously went about preparing a project or presentation for nine months only to be told, "That's disgusting, yuck, horrible, no, get out of here"?

A Safe Place to Dig

A dog's request is to give him a place to build his "sand castles." He needs a digging zone. Shape the digging. If you are lucky enough to have a puppy at eight weeks, begin by showing him where to dig. It's as simple as teaching "dig here, not there, dig for this, not that."

Make it a game of hunt and find. A plastic swimming pool filled with sand makes a great burial ground for bones and toys. Show him his favorite bone or hard rubber toy, make it enticing to him, then bury it in an acceptable and safe excavation spot. Voilà, jackpot! Take a walk with your dog around the yard and pick out an optimum cooling spot that he can build into a den to relax.

Don't want him in your vegetable or flower garden, and you don't have the time to teach him where to dig? Then, the answer is simple: fence it off.

Give Me a Job

Whether it's catching flying discs, playing ball, bringing you flowers, or fetching the newspaper, dogs were bred to work and need to feel useful. In addition to appropriate digging expeditions, give her a job to do in her daily life plan. You have choices, and it is worth the effort.

Does your dog fancy picking things up in her mouth? Like to retrieve? Enjoy rolling over? These activities are gems for your and your dog's creativity. Teach your dog to pick out a toy from his toy box and put it back. Pick up a children's basketball hoop and ball, teach the drop ... score. Bury the basketball, teach "go dig and find," then score through the hoop.

Though this seems extremely time-consuming, you can actually accomplish this in 10- to 15-minute sessions a couple of times a day. Yes, you absolutely can train your puppy using the concept we parrot regularly: "Do something for me and I'll do something for you!"

JUMPING

Contrary to what some might think, dogs do not sit down during the day and plot out a strategy for clouting their owners or visitors upon their arrival at the hacienda. They jump to extend their greetings of hello and because they have not been taught an alternative method for the greeting ritual. Greeting rituals are important to dogs. Watch them. They sniff, circle, sniff again, maybe hop on each other's backs, paw, sniff some more, and then they play, lie down, walk away, or have a quarrel.

✦ ✦ ✦

Dogs leap for a variety of reasons: joy, appeasement, greetings, for the sheer fun of it, and because it has been accepted by humans with a smile.

✦ ✦ ✦

Ironically, humans teach dogs that jumping is acceptable at a very early age. Puppies rise to the occasion to be near us. Most pups are rewarded continuously for pawing at us to say, "Hi there," to be touched, or taken outside.

We very often welcome this gesture of joyful greeting—that is, until someone gets slammed into a countertop, has his or her lap toasted by hot coffee, or even worse, gets knocked to the ground.

A dog's interpretation may sound like this: "Okay, by pawing or jumping, I usually achieve my goals for getting attention, to play, for food, to be picked up or massaged. Wow, apparently it's not acceptable anymore because I got bonked on the snout this time. I'm really confused. What the heck is the matter with this human? How come she is lying on the ground? That never happened before. Look at her face. I think I'm in trouble. I'm going now. I'll save me."

Dogs can be taught to jump up, with their paws on your shoulders, without plunging you through a wall at a mighty force that can only be experienced, not clearly illustrated. This picture illustrates a safe jumping technique with a request from a "sit" position, to an "up," then "off."

Gary lends a hand (and a cue) as Casidy demonstrates a safe and joyous jump. Unwanted behavior, such as jumping on people, can be shaped to more appropriate behavior. (Photo by Maureen Ross)

This is a classic example of putting a jump on cue, safely away from the human body. It's not advisable for children, and especially not with big dogs or without the supervision of adults. The safest approach with children is to teach them to have the puppy or dog sit before anything else.

✦ ✦ ✦

Teach your dog an acceptable and safe alternative to jumping, like sit or down, for social activity and requests (counterconditioning). Reward the automatic sits and downs.

✦ ✦ ✦

Cueing and Transitions

Let's take a moment to review cueing and transitions in relation to dog training. A cue is anything said or done that is followed by a specific action or response (voice or hand signal). A transition is movement or change from one position, behavior, stage, place, phase, subject, or concept to another.

Begin teaching puppies to sit or down on cue the moment they enter the human family home (a huge transition for a pup). It's easy, because puppies sit naturally by two weeks old. Begin shaping voluntary sits, rather than focus on the involuntary jumping. When the pup jumps or paws, gently request a sit by bringing a delicious piece of kibble or a treat in front of her muzzle, wiggling it, then bringing it over her head. The treat is a lure, not just a reward. It gets the pup's attention focused on you, so you can achieve a goal—sit—and 99.9 percent of the pups will sit down or roll over. So, probability is on your side here. Then, add your cue by requesting a sit or down. Work smart, not hard.

Be the Director of the Scene

Visualize all homecomings and visitations between your dog and friends, family members, or strangers on the street (be streetwise). Pretend that you are the "director" of the scene. How do you want this movie to begin, climax, and end? Factor in unpredictability, be flexible, and edit as you go along. What would be the optimal scenario? The doorbell rings and your pup, barking excitedly, leaps to the door; you request a sit before you open the door, and she sits.

Actors may do some improvising to their scripts, but they always have a "director" to ensure they give the best performance possible. Do this for your pup during social encounters. Direct everyone to gently request a sit from your pup before greeting rituals begin.

Changes in the Script?

Some actors have a chemistry and artistic ability that comes across on screen, making us cry, laugh, be frightened, and relate to, learn from, or thoughtfully reflect upon the scenes. Conversely, we have all experienced some movies that we wished we hadn't paid for! In a sense, this is the same for your dog. Every interaction between your pup and an individual or situation will be different, depending on how it's translated by the dog. Every interaction and response will depend on the past and present associations.

You can't control every nuance of activity that happens, but as a good director, you can make good use of creative freedom and see about changing the script.

Your pup may sit for you and other family members, but maybe not for Aunt Emma who bends over and in a cheery voice, says, "Come here, puppy, jump on Auntie Em's lap." If you really want this to turn out to be a good movie, direct Auntie Em to request a sit, then it's your choice whether she can pick up the pup or not. What kind of precedent will it set for future greetings? Are you planning a sequel to the movie entitled, "The Jumperator"?

Other Outtakes

Troubleshooting daily will ensure that your dog learns the difference between what's on- and off-limits. This extends throughout the dog's lifetime in many different scenes, including jumping on sofas, beds, tables, and countertops. Choose the pieces of furniture you will allow your dog to jump on. Want to cuddle on the couch to watch "Jumping on People" with Cuddles? Okay, then teach the up and off on "select" pieces of furniture. Dogs learn this easily. Clever dogs will choose their own pieces of furniture when you aren't looking, if the consequence in the past hasn't been one that helps them realize the difference.

Know that although dogs have keen eyesight, they may not discriminate between a peach-colored comforter and a navy blue one. A comforter is a comforter, period. If rainy, muddy paw prints are going to infuriate you on the peach comforter, better not teach "on the bed." An alternate approach (and there are many) would be to put Ranger's own comforter on the bed, or teach him to jump on the side to snuggle, and say, "Good night." Get the picture?

✦ ✦ ✦

"Always do right. This will gratify some people and astonish the rest!" —Mark Twain

✦ ✦ ✦

SEPARATION ANXIETY

Separation anxiety as defined in psychology is based on an infant's fear of losing its mother. In this sense it's understandable that separation anxiety is used as a catchall for any behaviors that happen when people leave their dogs home alone. However, it's an inaccurate assumption in most cases. There are true cases of separation anxiety that require treatment: a combination of behavior modification and sometimes medication (for humans and dogs).

To truly diagnose a dog with separation anxiety, however, requires careful assessment of the symptoms. Simple separation anxiety can be remedied with desensitization techniques, shaping the desired behaviors, and confinement to a safe haven when the owner is away.

Dr. Ian Dunbar relates in his article "Separation Fun" that "creating a Jekyl and Hyde environment produces a Jekyl and Hyde personality. The dog is happy as a clam when the owner is home, but upset and anxious when the owner is away. Different breeds and dogs are more dependent on their owners than others. Often, however, the dog's dependency is exacerbated by the necessities of the owner's lifestyle and unintentionally fostered by the owner's good intentions."

Dogs that are given an overabundance of affection and attention are likely to become anxious when affection is withdrawn. To take this a step further, we need to be mindful as human beings that it's not fair to endow upon the dog the job of filling in all the voids in our lives. Dogs usually offer us unconditional company, love, and affection when we are dealing with death, divorce, and other highly emotional transitions in life. Our responsibility as fair companions to our dogs is to endeavor to develop healthy coping mechanisms for them. Build up the dog's confidence level for lifestyle transitions, including being left home alone. Begin leaving your dog alone for short sessions (10 minutes at the most), increasing appropriately when you receive satisfactory results. All behavior-modification programs that involve desensitization should begin by slowly introducing the subject to the environment, or thing, that creates the anxiety. A good therapist would never throw a person who has a fear of spiders into a room full of arachnids, for example. Take it slow — it's more effective. Always praise a positive result and downplay any negative response from your dog.

"Separation fun" is the likely diagnosis for dogs left home for inordinately long periods of time without the necessary accoutrements to prevent them from being destructive. There's a reason for problem behaviors like chewing wallpaper, sofas, and underwear. If a dog does any of these, then he is not ready to be left roaming free within a house without supervision.

To learn, a dog needs to be taught that the specific behavior is inappropriate — and pronto. Delayed correction is insidious and addicting. Returning-home punishments simply do not work. The dog makes absolutely no connection to chewing the sofa and the owner's arrival and sudden anger. The dog simply did what came naturally. He was bored. He hadn't been taught to use chew toys and was punished before, so he got anxious approximately 30 minutes to one hour before the owner's arrival home. Chances are, at about the same time, he picked out a chair and chewed the arm to shreds. Why not? He anticipates punishment anyway and, believe it or not, chewing the chair is calming for him. This is probably his way of de-stressing before the big boom (you coming home). Get the picture?

Most dogs that display self-confidence during their owners' absence are probably completely thrilled to see them leave. They finally have a chance to be a dog with no human expectations. With the appropriate environment and entertainment, they blissfully enjoy separation fun.

Positive Problem Solving: Let's Brainstorm!

I. Identify the problem (specific):

II. Be creative and list options and possible solutions:

❑ _____

❑ _____

❑ _____

❑ _____

❑ _____

❑ _____

❑ _____

❑ _____

❑ _____

❑ _____

❑ _____

❑ _____

❑ _____

III. Check the boxes for those that sound reasonable to you.

IV. Write in the three "best" and why you chose them.

1. _____

2. _____

3. _____

V. Repeat Steps I, II, III, and IV once again and now decide on your plan.

Chapter Fifteen

Using Creative Games to Train

Learning about canine behavior can be so much fun if you integrate creative games into the teaching experience. Some people prefer regimented training. It has its advantages, particularly if you are a structured learner. We all have different areas in which we are stronger and other areas that need development (e.g., visual, audio, organizational, verbal or nonverbal performance). Many of us thrive on a blended learning style, utilizing a combination of these.

We designed *Train Your Dog, Change Your Life* to accommodate different styles of learning. We emphasized this at the beginning of the book and would like to do so again: Continue using the entire book while working your way through the lesson plans in Section Two. We encourage you to be creative and use your own style. Integrate some of these games, metaphors, and techniques with your own ideas to produce an individual, unique, and original repertoire that best suits your needs and those of your family and your dogs.

Be mindful that whichever way you choose to use this book. The main goal is to build a trusting relationship with your dog. The bonus is change for yourself, if you are ready. Imagine that you are holding a bunch of helium balloons in all different colors. Some are vivid, some are pale in color. You can let a balloon go any time you want with an undesired emotion or event in your life that you want to release. This includes behavior that your dog, in your mind's eye, doesn't live up to. Let those balloons go and blow up some new ones. You have alternatives, possibilities, and lots of resources for your dog's training and for yourself. Use them, make wise choices, and most of all learn from the experiences. Be in the present moment and allow your dog to enlighten you in the here and now. Enjoy the journey; you are responsible for the outcome of your relationship with your dog.

CROSS TRAINING

Cross training (CT) is an exciting and useful game. CT is best utilized when you and your dog have an understanding of the basics, like sit, down, stand, stay, and come-on-recall. (See the lessons in Section Two.) The definition of CT is similar to that of exercising, using a combination of step, aerobics, kickboxing, tai chi, pilates, treadmill, walking, rebounding, or yoga. CT is using either your voice or hand signals and to teach your dog the difference, thus increasing her repertoire. It makes training exhilarating.

The technical purpose is for proofing and reliability, or, as some trainers call it, shifting context. Does your dog know what "sit" is from your voice only? How about a sit from a hand signal only? If you place your dog in a stand-stay, then turn around with your back facing her, does she know what sit means when you make the request? Now try a hand signal. If you place your dog in a sit-stay and walk diagonally to the right or the left—either to the front or the back of the dog—and then request a heel, what does your dog do? Does "front" or "come" (given verbally and/or with a hand signal) mean from a sit-stay only? It shouldn't. Front, or any other request that has meaning or relevance to the dog, should be zealously responded to from anywhere, any place, at any time.

CT Benefits

Cross training provides:

- Proofing and reliability
- Distraction training
- Directional training
- Alternate communication possibilities (aging process)
- Alternatives for those with physical disabilities

We are not suggesting that it's a good idea to constantly change your daily routine, or your dog's, pronto, but it's essential, especially if you want to increase attention span and capability. It can add some spice to your lives, teaching you to be aware and flexible. Is it risky? Yes, it can be. Moving to a different location or adding a new stimulus (sight, sound, smell, body posture, challenge) will wake up both you and your dog. Integrating spontaneity, within reason, to your training program increases awareness and skill. It gives the dog the opportunity to work through the process of whatever task you give her, which can be fun for the dog if she truly enjoys what she's doing.

There are many combinations that you can orchestrate using CT. Begin slowly by first checking out what your dog already knows. Use hand signals alone, then voice signals. What are the results? Is the dog confused? Okay, then you know that you need to begin by slowly integrating hand and voice signals together, then eliminating one while requesting a sit, down, or stay. When the dog responds, praise.

We consider raising the criteria to different locations and adding distractions to be at an intermediate level. Every person and dog will progress at a different rate. You may find your dog loves the game of CT, but begin at the beginning, teaching both and then alternating one or the other. This will build a catalog of strong and diverse ways of communicating with your dog in a variety of situations.

WHISPER TRAINING

Words have little meaning to dogs until we teach them the concept associated with the meaning of the word. Then, they learn to listen for our words and watch for our body cues. Dogs respond to sights, sounds, smells, emotional energy, body language, and eye contact. If you have good communication strategies developed with your dog, then you will joyfully get the response you expect most of the time, while factoring in that nothing is ever perfect. You will feel better and more accomplished if you are realistic enough to allow for mistakes, and then learn from them.

Whispering is a delightfully peaceful alternative for your dog. Dogs have extremely keen hearing compared to humans. Shouting at a dog is like having a very loud horn blown in your face.

Whisper training is exactly like it sounds. You whisper the requests to the dog in a calm voice. The intention is to whisper with attitude. Heartily employ your facial expressions, changing them to fit the projected emotion (happy, sad, confused, displeased, try it again, and ecstatic). Your whisper inflection needs to vacillate a bit from stronger to softer in order to clarify the meaning of your request, with a corresponding hand signal that the dog is used to or is being taught. Honestly, your facial expressions and hand signals will say the most with or without the whisper. It just seems easier for us humans when we have something to do with our mouths.

Whisper training, accommodated with or without hand signals, can be as effective as a normal training tone of voice if practiced. The boon of whisper training is simply that it's a different approach and a quiet one. It gets the dogs curious as to what's coming next in a more natural way, while still giving us humans the opportunity to use our voices, which seems to be inherently habitual for most of us. You become an interesting focal point. Watch the dog's facial expressions the first time you try whispering. It's precious.

DANCE AND TRAIN

If you like Fred Astaire, Michael Jackson, or Ricky Martin, then tap-dance, moonwalk, or mambo la vida loca around the room. Hop on one foot and then the other, or swing dance. The idea is to be doing something different to challenge your dog's training ability, while getting some healthy exercise as a fringe benefit. The bonus is that the dogs love it when we are silly, because when we are silly, we're relaxed without expectations.

Don't let the dog miss out on all the fun. It will get pretty boring if all he gets to do is sit and watch his silly human hopping around on one foot. Include him when you are positive that you won't be setting him up for failure. Circling (or twirling) is a common routine in training exercises. Skip, sing, trot, or gallop around him instead of walking, ensuring that he maintains his sit-stay until you return to the front. Praise profusely—especially if he had to listen to you sing, too. Now have him twirl to the left, then to the right. This is easy using an enhanced food lure (something they really love). Bring the food lure in front of the muzzle, wiggle it, and bring it around in a circle. Later put a hand cue on this by twirling your index finger in a circle. Then reverse it.

There are many variations to dance routines, as you will see if you decide to get a freestyle video. Begin slowly, then increase the complexity and variations of the routines. The dog needs to know the basics as well as back-up, forward, go-through, and up-and-over. A safe and successful way to begin is to teach a back-up while heeling. Have your dog stop, remain standing, then prompt her with a food treat or hand signal to back-up with you, two or three steps at a time. This is a show-stopper when friends visit. "My dog can heel backwards, can yours?"

Take-a-bow is a favorite at Dog Talk. It's easy to teach by using an enticing food lure. Take the food lure, put it in front of the dog's muzzle and lower it slowly towards the floor. Anatomically and naturally the dog will move its head down toward the treat. Add in your cue of take-a-bow. When the dog does it on her own, or gives you a playbow, promptly say, "Yes, bravo, take-a-bow." You'll soon have a dog bowing all over the place, so put the behavior on cue. Then, you can manage it.

Beyond the sheer joy of integrating games, dancing, and music into training sessions is the inevitable reality that your dog will eventually be exposed to all of these anyway, especially if he lives with children. Dogs are going to encounter people of different cultures dancing, children laughing and screaming, all in a variety of environments. So, why not take the initiative and introduce these activities to the dog yourself in advance? Throw on a stovepipe hat. Dogs sense when you are lightening up and being silly. It creates a relaxing reprieve to a humdrum training routine, while desensitizing them to all sorts of strange objects. And, you'll have fun doing it.

Music is a matter of preference. Obviously, if you are relaxing and training, you want to use tranquil music. Tranquil music will help you both breathe and de-stress. Playing music when you leave your dog alone can be soothing. For more excitement or to practice jolly-ups and settle-downs, play some rock-and-roll or country. Our recommendation is to end all training sessions with relaxation, a deep breath, and a dog-hug. We do this in class, sending people and their dogs home pleasantly calm.

DOG TEAM GAMES

You can easily integrate games into your training repertoire with your family a couple of times a week. Be mindful that like with any game, there are rules. We can't emphasize that enough. You are aware now and realize that you need to set guidelines, start and stop games, and watch out for overly enthusiastic dogs that may cross that threshold into being disruptive or destructive. Know the thresholds and manage them. When children and dogs are put together in a game-playing venue, the safest way is the supervised way. Have fun, but maintain some balance and harmony in the pack (humans and dogs) by managing appropriate levels of excitement.

Hide-and-Seek

Imagine the look on your dog's face when she is asked to find a family member or a bone? We have all played hide-and-seek, so include your dog in on the fun. Dogs rely on routine, so hide a biscuit at night before bedtime and have them "go-find." Say, "Good dog" and then, "Good night."

Musical Chairs

This is another self-explanatory game that we all played as children. This works best with more than one dog, but the family can use variations of this with one dog. Put one family member in charge of the music. Have each family member take turns with the dog. Play the music and when it stops, well, you know the rules ... everyone has to be in a chair. The dog team has to have the dog sitting or in a down-stay.

Walk a Mile in My Paws

This is a training game that can be done with clickers, too. The human has to be the dog, while other humans train that person (using either a click or praise) to do a previously decided-upon task, like walking through the kitchen and touching the basket. It sounds easy, but try it and you will see how confusing it can be for a puppy to be given multiple requests by several people. It's analogous to playing charades.

Tail-Wagging Game

Who can get the dog to wag his or her tail on cue? We do this one in class all the time, and especially for adopted dogs who are stressed or fearful, because we want to encourage people and dogs to enjoy training. When a dog's tail is wagging east and west (not north or south) we know they are comfortable and having fun. If a dog is willing to take a treat, we know they aren't overly stressed.

Simon Says

This fun game requires everyone to concentrate on listening and responding to simple requests from the designated "Simon" asking for a "sit" or "down." Again, we play this in class, but families can use variations of this game at home by giving each person (or child) a chance at playing the game while being responsible for the puppy, too.

Target Games

Target games can be played with just the two of you (one person, one dog). Clickers are great for teaching target games. You need to introduce yourself to clicker training to understand the concept, but you can use the praise or treat method, too. (Read Chapter Sixteen, "Clicker Training," and pick up Karen Pryor's book *A Dog and a Dolphin* or her videos on clicker training.) When we click/treat, we add a voice applause like "yes" or "bravo" to use alternately when we do not have a clicker. This is an easy and useful connection that does absolutely no harm to the training process. The dog associates with and learns well from both, whether used together or separately.

Target games can begin by touching his nose with a finger, a wand, or a broomstick. This can extend to a wide range of items that it will be useful to teach your dog to approach gently, such as a door, a lap, a child's hand, a wheelchair arm (pet-assisted therapy), or the side of a bed (for a visit). This is the same technique that assistance dogs are taught when they're required to touch phones (ringing for hearing-impaired person) or open and close doors.

Chicken Dog Retrieve

Use chicken dogs cut into small chunks, or if you are opposed to human food for treats, toss your dog's favorite stuffed thingy through your legs next time you call "come." Have them go through your legs. Be careful with giant breeds ... you can get tossed!

Diagonals, Circles, Cones, and Bushes

This game is a great way to teach your dog directions and how to pace with you on a loose leash or an off-leash walk. With your dog in a sit, down, or stand-stay, walk diagonally to the left, right, or backwards to the left and right. Request a heel. On walks, circle around, go through trees and bushes, and have him touch traffic cones (check for traffic first). Make it seem like something that you really desire. Show him your enthusiasm and interest in him touching a bush. You can extend this to so many other important items.

The Dog Swap

All puppies and dogs should be confident in knowing that if you leave them with someone—whether at a friend's place, a relative's home, or a boarding kennel—you'll be back. If you have a strong relationship with your dog, there should be no question in your dog's mind that you'll be back.

You can begin in training class. If your instructors aren't using this technique, suggest it and explain why. Pick another dog team, swap dogs, and take a walk.

Cheerfully, but not with overwhelming emotion, leave your pup for a couple of hours with a friend ("see you later"); then extend to an overnighter. Your dog will soon learn that goodbye doesn't mean forever. Most dogs, much to our chagrin, have a ball when we leave anyway.

The Dog Tether

Remember the good ol' western flicks where the cowboy gallantly rides into town and tethers his horse to a hitching rail? Ever see the horse panic? Not if it were Trigger, Roy Rogers's noble steed. Create a noble dog by desensitizing him. Tether him for short amounts of time to a hitch or doorknob. This will be valuable at the veterinarian's office while you pay your bill and get your instructions for medications. It's handy at parks, events, or anywhere you may have to use your hands.

Tethering teaches the dog that he can momentarily and safely be left alone, whether in or out of your presence, without having kittens. Your relationship with your dog should be confident enough that he can be securely left without exhibiting signs of unjustified stress. This, by no means, suggests that any dog should be left unsupervised for unreasonable lengths of time anywhere (e.g., outside of stores, in the back of a pick-up truck, or at shopping malls).

OUTDOOR GAMES

For economic reasons, it behooves us all to invent outdoor apparatuses to amuse our little geniuses. Our American Bulldog, Casidy, needs an outlet to channel her creative energy, so we built her an up-and-over that she likes to go up and jump off. The ramps now double as a walk-up to the swimming pool. Our Newfs love to pull their carts and jump through truck tires. Hula-Hoops are great for go-throughs, too. Old broomsticks can be utilized for over-and-under.

A plastic swimming pool is a source of entertainment and a cool spot on hot summer days. Plastic pools can become warm, cozy beds in the winter with a few imitation lambskins or polar fleece added for comfort. They can be filled with sand and used to bury dog bones for search-and-find, and turned upside down for an alternate "find-it" game (biscuits/bones/toys).

OVERWORKED AND UNDERPLAYED

We have all used the phrase "overworked and underpaid." It's time to consider the effects of being overworked and underplayed. As Dr. Richard Carlson shares in *Don't Sweat the Small Stuff*, "unless you know something that we don't know, when you die you will leave your home and all your possessions behind." Despite this rather obvious observation, many of us fail to live as if this were true. Instead, we spend a huge amount of time and energy tending to dusting, caring for, purchasing, insuring, protecting, taking care of, and showing off our stuff, all as if it had some lasting value. This isn't to say that we don't deserve or shouldn't honor our stuff when it brings us joy, as long as it does bring us joy and has some intrinsic meaning for us. Our dogs bring us true joy. Rediscover your discovery zone with the help of your dogs.

Work, work, and no play makes for a dull day. Choosing to share our lives with dogs and children can teach us valuable lessons. Dogs and kids have always known what adults need to relearn: chill-out, play, and learn something new every day.

Training Guidelines

If training is a game, then here are the rules:

- Take a deep breath and exhale.
- Organize, plan, implement, understand that things change, make the change
- Be proactive, rather than reactive (plan, prevent, provide).
- Be fair, fun, flexible, and forgiving.
- Problem-solve, set goals, negotiate conflict fairly.
- Keep it safe and interactive, with guidelines.
- Be enthusiastic (a motivator) and develop a sense of humor.
- Use your ABC's (Antecedent + Behavior = Consequence).
- Set short- and long-term realistic, achievable, flexible goals.
- Do something for me and I'll do something for you (be your dog's best friend).
- Give the dog a chance to learn and the space to be a dog.
- Reframe and relocate (make a shift from one location or training routine to another).
- Catch your dog in the act of doing something right.
- Be accountable for the outcomes.
- Again, take a deep breath, release, renew, relax, let go, and grow. Enjoy your relationship with your dog!

Have you ever observed dogs at play? It's pure entertainment.

They get down with attitude, roll on the ground, kick their feet and legs, and get their jollies. When bored, which is a lot of the time for dogs, they creatively find ways to entertain themselves.

PLAY TRAINING

You can train while you play. This is an event that the whole family can enjoy. Play sessions should be timed; that is, short periods of any of the games listed in this chapter. Each game must have a beginning and an end.

A Poodle leaps on command. Don't forget that playtime can be training time—learning happens all the time. (Photo by Winter/Churchill Photography)

Playing Tug-of-War

Tug-of-war games should be supervised. Dogs love to tug because it satisfies their urge to pull, tear, and chew. Here's the key: You (the adult) begin and end the game. You (not the dog) choose the toy. Set the limits of "how hard" to play. Children should not play tug-of-war until they are capable of understanding this concept. Otherwise, choose safer games to play. There are plenty of them.

CHILDREN AND GAME PLAYING

Children need to be supervised and taught how to play with dogs safely and gently. Being a strong role model is essential. Under adult supervision, young children can learn to teach one play behavior at a time.

The rules should be fair: "You do something for me, like sit-wait, and I'll do something for you, like throw the ball or get your flying disc for a great energy-draining game of chase-and-bring-back." With this approach, you are integrating training into play while teaching the children how to play without overstimulating the pup. You're also teaching respect for another species, and this can be taken either way: dog to human or human to dog. The dog learns a safe, win-win way to do one of the things that motivates them the most—play!

THE DOG WALK

Walking is a healthy exercise for you and your dog. It's a great way to train, particularly if you have a busy lifestyle.

Why walk? For most of us it's a natural way of getting from one place to another. Many people believe that dogs get enough exercise running with other dogs in the backyard, in their kennels, or on cable runs. It's marvelous that dogs get to romp safely in fenced-in yards with other companion dogs. However, these are not the dogs or the stimuli that they will encounter on everyday walks, with the veterinarian, with the groomer, or at the park.

Walk the Walk

Apart from the obvious, the purpose and relevance of frequent walks for you and your dogs are:

• To socialize puppies to strangers, cars, children, and other dogs so she will not be frightened as an adult (teach her to be streetwise).

• To familiarize her to all sorts of potentially frightening environmental stimuli and sounds.

• To get exercise.

Training on Walks

Dogs are used to familiarity, like a "sit" at home for their dinner, greeting guests, and in training class. The key is to bring them out on a walk. Have them sit-down-and-stay for a few minutes in several different locations. Teach them to trust you. While on a walk, stop and train your dog every 20 yards or so. In just a one-mile walk you can integrate many different training elements, such as sit, down, stay, wait, slow, fast, and normal walk. Walk around trees, bushes, and groups of people. Try not to incite fear by being anxious yourself. Take a deep breath and push your pause button (one, two, three) ... exhale.

Use a tone of voice that is consistent and appropriate for the particular scenario. You are having a pleasant walk, so don't be tense. When requesting a behavior, a soft but firm tone is best. Dogs have excellent hearing. It's your presentation of the request that makes the difference. Use an encouraging voice when the dog is doing well, praise and reward, or simply say, "Okay, that's very nice." Be calm when you expect calmness and vice versa.

If you are doubtful about an oncoming situation (for example, another dog/owner team approaching), then veer off and let it go for the time being. Respond to your dog's request to arc to the side. The dog knows what he is doing. He senses something is not quite right, so honor that movement. Don't get stressed. Your dog will immediately pick up your emotions. His senses are much more acute then ours.

Fun, Easy, Healthy

Walking and training should be kept in perspective. Integrate the training sequences into the walk without becoming obsessive-compulsive about it. Leave some time for play. Remember to praise when your dog offers you a behavior that is special.

Enthusiasm and reliability will improve dramatically if you integrate training with walking. Dogs like to know what's expected and relevant. Bring along your dog's favorite ball or tug toy. When you have a delightful, no-pull, loose-leash walk, either praise and reward or toss the ball.

If your dog becomes confused or overzealous, simply take away the reward—cease the walk and/or turn away. Try Zen: Be a tree. The walk itself becomes the motivator. When the dog is by your side and calm, then resume the walk.

Walking is a marvelous way to impress onlookers, meet people, get healthy, train, and have fun with your dog. Of the many advantages, the very best is just getting out there and spending time building a trusting and understanding relationship. You are giving yourself a gift and your dog a chance to sniff.

Due to busy lifestyles, a large majority of dogs relish the daily walk. An opportunity to run "free" means exploration and yahoo time. It's pure entertainment. They get to venture into the unknown. You may be positive about your dog's reliability, but you can never be sure about the zillions of other possibilities that the environment will present.

Don't assume that everyone wants to play with your puppy, especially another dog.

Enjoy walking and hiking with your dogs. Do it in a healthy, respectable, and safe way for all concerned. Set a good example for other dog walkers and children. Bring your dog-bags to pick up after your dog. The next time you walk and train with Livingston, sing Aretha Franklin's tune "Respect, just a little bit" along the way as a reminder. Expect some respect from others too. You deserve it.

Chapter Sixteen

Clicker Training

A clicker is a great device to train new behaviors. A clicker produces an auditory signal, like praise or a whistle, that is crisp, distinctive, and clear. For those who hesitate with verbal praise, clickers can improve timing. Clickers and praise are conditioned reinforcers, signals that tell your dog that you like a behavior. Unconditioned reinforcers are treats, food, petting, your attention, or any other pleasure; something the dog would want, or more than likely get, even without training.

The Click

There is nothing inherently rewarding about clicks or praise. They must be associated with the real reward: treat, pet, play, games. The click becomes a predictor for the dog, telling him that a treat or play is imminent. He learns to like and work for the click, which means food or play.

Jackpot!

When you get your jackpot (a great and specific behavior), convey your enthusiasm by adding multiple treats and praise, after the click. These events should be rare. Otherwise, you will lose clicking and treat momentum.

CLICKER-TRAINING TIPS

Get yourself a clicker and a few small, tasty treats. To avoid boredom or to increase motivation, vary the reward that follows the click: kibble, string cheese, chicken dogs, Oinker Rolls, low-fat kielbasi, a walk, a tummy rub, a game of hide-and-seek, liver treats.

Begin by clicking and treating to demonstrate to your dog what the meaning and sound of "click" is. Then do this in different parts of the room or yard four or five times. Then, click and delay the treat for a few seconds. If the dog actively looks for the treat, you know the signal (click) has become a conditioned reinforcer.

The clicker has great value in shaping new behavior or refining details; it's not necessary in exhibiting behavior that the dog has already learned, like a sit. It can refine an okay sit to a flashy, quick sit aligned perfectly by your side, if that's what your goal is. There's no cookbook recipe for developing behavior because each training session is different. You have to wing it, be creative, and use your imagination by adding ingredients along the way. That's what is so much fun about clicker training.

Click first, then treat. Always click while the behavior is happening. The click sound is like an arrow that goes right into the dog's nervous system with the message, "What you are doing at this instant has just paid off." The timing is crucial to tell the dog exactly what you liked. If you click all over the place, the dog will try out a repertoire of many behaviors, but never become reliable at the one you specifically want to shape. As mentioned previously, we prefer to add praise with the click. The dogs pair click and praise together easily, and you're covered if you don't have your clicker. Expressing praise is something you can do anytime, anywhere.

Don't use your clicker to get your dog's attention. If you choose to do this, then don't use it for teaching other behaviors. If you use the clicker as a distraction from the environment or to get your dog to come, it will lose its power of information for the dog. To teach come, for example, show your dog the delicious treat he might get, place him somewhere in a sit, stand, or down, then call your dog. As soon as you get your dog's attention, click and treat. If the dog doesn't come, then toss a morsel of the treat to the dog. Try again from a few feet away. If you receive a head turn and a couple of steps toward you, click and treat. After five or six reinforcements, even a cautious dog will join you. This can be effectively used in the reverse direction, teaching your dog to "go to your mat or dog napper." The minute the dog creates a footpath toward the napper, click and treat, throwing the morsels closer and closer to the napper. You can use their favorite toys, too.

Don't use your clicker for encouragement or as a start signal. For example, if your dog lags behind you and you click, you are reinforcing the lagging. If your dog hesitates and you click, you are reinforcing the hesitation. Click only for the behavior you want. When your dog is walking comfortably by your side, click and treat. Then, over a series of brief sessions, challenge yourself and the dog by changing speed and direction. You get the idea.

Click for success. Don't bag the whole process over one mistake. Go back to kindergarten. If your dog even looks at you, click and treat. Always end on a positive note, or just end, but never stop a training session in a huff. If you are all stressed out, chances are your dog is, too. There is miscommunication happening here.

SHAPING (TARGETING)

Now that you have your dog accustomed to the clicker, you can establish a behavior. It's wise to pick a behavior that the dog does not already know. Visualize a behavior that you desire. You can start with a simple request to "touch" your finger. When you receive a touch, click and treat. The treat must follow the click to be effective. Try "touch" to your finger again (targeting). When the dog touches, click and treat. Do this several times. Now, hold out your finger and say "touch." If the dog touches, click and treat. Try again, but this time do not say "touch." If your dog touches: no click, no treat, just a "tough luck" or "too bad." Why? Because you did not request a "touch." This is what teaches the difference. Then, of course, "try again."

When your dog has learned a new behavior, now you can begin clicking for every second response, then every few. This is integrating a variable reinforcement schedule into click and treat. It actually builds stronger behavior because the dog is now anticipating the next click and treat. It increases attention span.

Training should be in short bursts. Three or four sessions, each five minutes long, will be more effective than three half-hour-long sessions where both you and the dog become exhausted or bored to tears. Behaviors enthusiastically trained by shaping and reinforcement do not deteriorate. Two or three quality behaviors are better than four or five sloppy ones.

Sometimes learning hits a plateau where the dog doesn't seem to "get it." Don't panic. Regress and start over. Plateaus are a gift because they usually are followed by a huge leap forward.

To summarize, don't click to fix or cease a behavior. Teach a more appropriate behavior. This can sound confusing, but it really isn't. By teaching the new behavior, this will, in many cases, automatically modify the old one. The clicker is designed for starting behavior, not for stopping it. In this context, clickers can work well for behavior modification or rehabilitation.

Section Four

The Rest of Your Journey

Relationship training is a lifelong program about awareness and education, as well as developing, nurturing, and maintaining a relationship. Now you're building the foundation to a reliable, rewarding, respectful, understanding, and enjoyable interdependent relationship with your canine companion. We invite you to extend everything you are learning with your dog to other aspects of your life.

As with life in general, the lessons are on a continuum. Learning and training are perpetual processes that are integral parts of day-to-day living. Whatever your goals in life are, the basic skills of problem solving, communication, conflict resolution, goal setting, and developing relationships are necessary elements for survival. Continue to develop these skills, explore areas of change, and teach your children the relevance of these skills and what we can all learn from nature, particularly our dogs.

In this final section, we'll explore issues that you'll encounter on the rest of your journey. In Chapter Seventeen, "Managing Your Dog and Your Life," we'll examine how to incorporate training into your family's busy schedule and explore ideas for personal renewal for dog owners. This section concludes with Chapter Eighteen, "Final Words of Wisdom," which provides a few thoughts for you to take with you as you enjoy your life with your dog.

Enjoy the rest of the journey. Be well and please, take care of yourself, your family, and your dogs. Respect nature. We invite you to read on for some more exciting, and what we hope will be helpful, sharing of experiences. The suggested readings offer a range of expertise that you may find beneficial.

Chapter Seventeen

Managing Your Dog and Your Life

Dog owners are literally bombarded with so many new training tools, techniques, books, and videos that it can be overwhelming. Raising a puppy or an older adopted dog can be fun and easy with some helpful resources. On the other hand, it can leave us walking around bookstores in circles. We come home from workshops equipped with every imaginable new gadget to help us teach our pups. All of this leaves the puppies and humans breathless. Most humans do not inherently have the coordination, timing, and dexterity to use all of this stuff anyway.

Honestly, pups learn quite naturally. They do not really care one scrap if we have spent a thousand bucks on expensive training tools or choose to tie old sweatshirt sleeves together in knots for play toys. All they need to know is: "What belongs to me to play with?"

Keep things in perspective. The same rules apply to both training our puppies and managing a business, organization, or family unit. More often than not, less is better. The key is to keep an open mind and use what works best for you, your family, and your pup. Everyone has a different reality, learning style, and limitations. Every human and pup is a unique and different individual. Within this reality come many hours of struggling over what is right or wrong. Just forget about it. Take a breath and listen to your intuition. If you already have a strong and healthy set of values, just ask yourself what works best. Does it feel right? Follow the simple and effective tried-and-true plan used to accomplish any project, whether small or large.

Four Rhodesian Ridgeback puppies are a handful for anyone. The key to raising a new puppy is to keep an open mind and use what works best for you, your family, and your pup. (Photo by Mary Bloom)

All families (in any species) have core values, beliefs, cultures, and family patterns. Adding a pup to the household can thrust the status quo into upheaval. Using a word, phrase, or saying that helps you associate one thing to another can remind you of the steps needed to manage your new pup or your house, business, and basically anything else you set your mind to.

You can make up your own word, but we recommend the word OPIUM (Organize, Plan, Implement, Understand, Make).

- Organize
- Plan (but don't get lost in your plan—enjoy the process)
- Implement the plan
- Understand that the best-laid plans are subject to change
- Make the change

Organize ahead of time! Most people who read this book will already have a pup. Allow us the privilege of being optimistic, as we enjoy giving people the benefit of the doubt. Perhaps you can be an ambassador and pass your learning experiences on to prospective new puppy owner wannabes. Let's just say you have done the following basics. The organizing (thinking about it) should happen before a puppy or adult dog joins your family and household. It's essential to sit down and be realistic with yourself (if you are alone), with a significant other, or with the family to discuss the responsibilities of buying and caring for a pup. While brainstorming, prepare a journal that includes finances, responsibilities, size, breed, adoption, location, how far you're willing to travel, and most importantly, your current lifestyle. Can a pup fit in it for at least 15 years? This is essential.

Just as adding a baby to your life is a life-altering experience, so is adding a puppy. Parents: Lessons on how to respect life and all of the species with whom we share the earth will be highlighted when a puppy joins your family. What a great way to be role models to your children by teaching them how to care for, gently train, and play with a puppy!

Plan. Great, you have agreed with yourself, a significant other, or the family that yes, absolutely, adding a pup is the thing to do. The plan involves preparing the house, family, friends and you for the arrival. Chapters One, Five, and Fourteen are invaluable. The self-help exercises will remind you that we all must take accountability for our choices.

Implement the Plan. Dogs are wonderful companions for children and adults. In our opinion, because they are such social creatures, including them as part of the family pack makes it easier to train them. That is why we at Dog Talk and Thera*Pet* make every effort to "capture the whole family" by having them join our classes. It is germane for everyone to participate in a safe environment with appropriate boundaries between dogs and humans.

Do your homework, ask your veterinarian, and join a puppy-training class. It should be motivating, supportive, and most importantly use positive techniques, especially with puppies. An effective learning environment includes more than just training techniques. It's a blend of people, sights, sounds, smells, and learning experiences. Competent and knowledgeable leaders coach and teach beyond basic training. They take it to the next level by using observations of body language (dogs' and humans'), communication, solution finding, and conflict-resolution skills as part of the teaching repertoire. They encourage you to look at yourself in relation to your pup.

A good metaphor for learning about dog language and training is to picture yourself being parachuted into a foreign country, beginning a new job, or starting college. What would it be like for you? Is it confusing, scary, and daunting? An immediate reaction and priority would be survival. This is species-inclusive. We all develop defense mechanisms to survive. You would not hesitate for a nanosecond to seek out ways to communicate and plan a strategy to figure out how to survive in a foreign environment. Puppies and dogs thrust into new environments do the exact same thing. They try to figure out what's safe or dangerous, pleasurable or not so. Like us, they make mistakes. What happens when they make mistakes leaves a lasting impression that will affect future relationship development.

Understand that the best-laid plans are subject to change. You are meticulous in your planning. Everything is in place—the crate, the dishes. The plan for family responsibilities is working well; exercise, good nutrition, grooming, and your veterinarian are terrific. House-training is coming along just fine. You arrive home and for some reason the house looks as if an insane person has vandalized it. You see your six-month-old pup chewing on a delicious piece of spongy inner sofa cushion. Under any other circumstance, this would be really cute. He has had a delightfully full day of entertainment. He is rather tired, has to eliminate, and wants his dinner. He is overjoyed that you have finally arrived home. What do you do?

If you are reading this book, you know that you can do absolutely nothing when that pup gleefully comes running with ears flopping to greet you, but to greet him right back with a smile. Put down the brief-case, grocery bags and take a deep breath. Take the pup out for a pee, feed him, and then proceed to the refrigerator door to check and see if the Family Puppy Planner disappeared. Whose turn was it to take care of the puppy? Was the crate door latched properly? Was he confined adequately in his own sanctuary or did someone decide to allow the pup to run loose? We all know by now that he shouldn't have been running around the house loose, right?

This is but one example of life's unpredictability. One thing we are 150 percent positive about is that none of us are 100 percent perfect. Life is always subject to change, just like New England weather. If something has gone awry, there is a reason. We guarantee it. It doesn't mean that chewing the sofa is okay; it does mean that you need to take a look at how the plan fell apart. Have a family meeting and reflect on what happened. Don't dwell on it—just process the day's events to understand what happened. Remember, even the best-laid plans may require change.

Make the change. You have had your family discussion and are considering solutions, or have made the necessary changes to prevent this occurrence in the future. If you live alone, then we have to assume you have picked up a mirror and had a reflective chat with yourself.

It is not the pup's fault for doing what comes naturally. This applies to every single incident as we learn from our experiences and build a trusting relationship, whether it is with dogs, children, people of different cultures, or Martians.

Families should work together for the learning experience, with Mom or Dad at the helm. The only way to do this is to join a family-oriented training program. Set aside a small amount of time everyday (10 minutes at breakfast and dinner) to review your list of who does what with the pup: when, where, how, and how many times a day. It must be flexible, fun, fair, and forgiving (the four F's) for everyone. Only gentle, positive training methods should be employed, and particularly when children are at the other end of the leash.

A SAMPLE FAMILY PACK

Let's improvise. The Cuddles Family—Mom, Dad, and two children ages five and eight—have added a new member to their pack, a Newfoundland puppy. Sailor is 10 weeks old and enrolled in basic training to begin in a few weeks (after his vaccinations and rabies shot). The trainer was referred by the Cuddles' veterinarian because she encourages the whole family to join the class with Sailor.

Mrs. Cuddles is advised by the trainer to socialize Sailor and sends her some preliminary reading material to get the family started. The trainer enthusiastically engages Mrs. Cuddles in a conversation about getting Sailor and family members on a schedule for feeding, walking, exercise, and elimination. She recommends one or two up-to-date positive-approach training books to give the Cuddles family a few choices and ideas about puppy planning and housetraining before they begin class. The trainer recommends having a puppy party to introduce Sailor to friends and neighbors, but to be sure that everyone has Sailor sit before petting him or giving him a treat.

Address the Real Problem

All the well-meaning advice in the world won't amount to a hill of dog bones if we're not addressing the real problem. And, we'll never get to the problem if we're so caught up in our own paradigm that we don't take off our glasses long enough to see the world from another's point of view (like our dogs').

The Sample Puppy Planner in this chapter can be torn out, reproduced, or modified to fit your needs. Post it on the refrigerator at the children's eye level. Make it a family task, something that is fun to do. Fill in the name of the person(s) responsible for each day, or week, whatever you decide. As an added bonus, you can begin, or include this in, an allowance (incentive) program for children. It can be made part of their daily tasks as being members of a family.

Obviously, with small children, adults will have to supervise activities. Keep it simple and achievable for them. Usually children around 12 and older can do just about all the puppy tasks. Coach them at least daily. You'll know when something isn't working because the puppy's behavior will send out clear warnings like SOS signals. The behavior, whether peeing on the floor or chewing (whatever is unacceptable to you), is showing signs that the family plan needs to be tweaked. Somebody isn't doing his or her job of supervising the puppy. Tear out your Positive Problem Solving exercise (in Chapter Fourteen); write down what the problem is and list the possible solutions.

Feeding time is a matter of preference, but we strongly recommend a schedule and so do most veterinarians. Let's consider that the puppy is being fed morning and evening. If so, then fill in whose responsibility it is to feed the pup. With children, ensure that they understand the appropriate amounts of food and emphasize no scraps or candy because "puppies don't brush their teeth and it isn't good for them." Puppies should always have access to water, but it's fine to pick it up in the evening, for example, after 8:00 P.M. This will ensure that after the last puppy-run outside, chances are you will have a good night's sleep.

Where you feed the pup is a matter of preference, and food time can be a great opportunity to train: sit-wait, "Good puppy, here's your food."

To summarize elimination schedules, the basic rule of thumb, particularly with puppies, is just that: Keep them on schedule. Up to about six months, puppies cannot hold their bladders for more than a few hours at a time. This clearly depends on what the puppy is doing as well. They need to eliminate when they wake up, about 20 minutes after eating, and immediately when you notice that they are curious or circling. If you are uncertain and, without turning into a door person, when in doubt, take them out.

Playtime can be integrated into potty time for those with busy lifestyles. It's beneficial to allow the pup to play a few minutes after eliminating. Otherwise, she will not learn to eliminate on cue, as she knows that this means, back in the house and probably the crate.

Exercise is healthy and relevant for growing pups. The best exercise is walking a couple of times a day. Free roaming, supervised exercise is excellent, particularly in a fenced dog park with other pups, but this can be time-consuming, and facilities hard to find. Wherever you exercise with your pup, be mindful of traffic and letting him run loose. He will explore, and it can get unsafe. Keep it in perspective.

In the house, be careful on slippery floors because the pup's bones are developing. Pups who are left outside (with supervision only) with children playing will often come in and urinate in the house. The pup and the children do not know any better, but the pup can be taught that after play, it's time to urinate, then time to come in.

Let's review sleeping arrangements for the pup. Puppies should sleep in a confined area where they can be safe and secure. We recommend crates in the bedroom, either yours or one of the children's. Dogs are social by nature and will cry less, particularly in the first week, if they can see their people. The puppy will need to go out every four hours or so, although some people are lucky enough to have the pup sleep through the night. What he has in their sleeping den is a matter of choice, but less is better. A blanket or towel and an indestructible toy like a Kong or Chewman will keep them company in the wee hours of the morning.

Along with a positive training program, unleash your creativity by making lists that are applicable to your lifestyle. Most training can be easily integrated into daily living.

A SAMPLE PUPPY PLANNER

Puppy's Name: _____

Date:	Sun.	Mon.	Tues.	Wed.	Thur.	Fri.	Sat.
Feeding							
Potty Time							
Playtime							
Exercise							
Time-Outs							
Sleeping Arrangements							
Training							

✦ ✦ ✦

"God grant me the Serenity to accept the things I cannot change

The Courage to change the things I can

and the Wisdom to know the difference."

—The Serenity Prayer

✦ ✦ ✦

PERSONAL RENEWAL FOR DOG OWNERS

Personal renewal is an important component of relationship training. Meditation is one way to renew yourself. During meditation, you can rest more deeply than when you sleep. It eases stress and is good for your health. It helps to put the everyday chaos of life into perspective.

Many people believe that for meditation to be useful, they have to sit like a pretzel and chant for long periods of time. Buddhist monks will do this, but we certainly can enjoy the benefits of meditation in a modified form to calm our frenetic lifestyles. If you want to sit cross-legged, fine. All you really need to do is just do it. Sit or lie quietly, breathe deeply, and let your thoughts flow easily. You can meditate wherever you are, when you have the time, and wherever you go. Just pick a quiet spot and retreat to your own created sanctuary. Use your imagination.

Meditation can take three minutes or a year (if you have the time). The only mistake you can make meditating is to force yourself. You really need to relax to achieve a state of restful awareness. Thoughts and subtle sensations will flow around you. You may experience internal imagery and sound effects. One moment you will be blissfully relaxing on a quiet beach, and the next, thinking about taking your dog for a walk. It's an opportunity to quietly sort through your thoughts and review emotions, including anger and fear. It's when we take the time to quiet our minds that these emotions flood us. It can be scary, but very "freeing" once put into perspective. Issues you are dealing with will become clearer. This clarity will help you to resolve these issues. This is a good time to reflect, renew, let go, and glow.

Along with meditation, we all need to look for some form of personal renewal or revival. Here are four areas to keep in balance when you get frazzled that will help enable you to regain energy, focus, and clarity:

1. **Physical:** Take a deep breath, healthy nutrition, exercise, manage stress.

2. **Mental:** Take a deep breath, balance, visualize, relax, set priorities.

3. **Spiritual:** Meditate, read, write in a journal, take nature walks (the mind, body, and spirit rely on each other for a confident and calm sense of well-being).

4. **Social/Emotional:** Build friendships, listen empathetically with an open mind.

✦ ✦ ✦

Stressed is desserts spelled backwards ... take it one bite at a time. ...

✦ ✦ ✦

Choosing to Be Centered

- Allows you to be more authentic, sensitive, and open.
- Produces emotional and physical stability.
- Has a positive effect on relationships and the surrounding environment.
- Has a great impact on developing trust.
- Enables you to appreciate the nature of conflict.
- Brings you to a point of clarity, the point of empowerment.
- Is always your choice, at any time...
- Conflict isn't good or bad. It's what we do with it that makes the difference.

Take a Deep Breath

Take a deep breath and for a moment, picture yourself parachuting into a foreign country without any knowledge of the language or culture ... intimidating, isn't it? What would you do to survive? Chances are, you would be pretty stressed out. Your breathing would accelerate and your body chemistry would soar. You may experience a full-blown panic attack that sends your body into a flight, fright-freeze, or appease response. At the very least, you would quickly learn how to communicate in any way possible, soon discovering that some methods of communication are acceptable, while others can be quite offensive.

This is similar to what puppies and adult dogs experience when learning how to communicate and survive in a human world. The response that sends our bodies, as humans, into a panic mode happens to dogs, too. They become stressed. Their blood chemistry changes. Under more serious and/or traumatic circumstances, it can take days (at least three), weeks, or months for a dog to calm down and for his biochemistry to return back to normal.

Be aware that dogs have acutely keen senses. Truthfully, they view the world through wide-angle lenses. Your dog will also interpret every nuance of your emotional change, facial expressions, and body movements. The level of training, understanding, and awareness that has developed can make a difference on how your dog interprets, reacts, or responds to these changes. Training with awareness of what you are communicating will help to develop a respectful and trusting relationship between you and your dog.

How Do I Do This?

Begin each training session by taking a deep breath. This act immediately reduces stress, helping you to focus. Throughout your training sessions, taking deep breaths can release tension and open up a mindful awareness of what is happening around you. This calmness will automatically affect your dog's attitude. If possible, get that tail wagging immediately, as training should be a sought-after and fun experience.

This is helpful in all situations throughout your day. One deep, cleansing breath will work wonders ... two, three, or four are even more effective. Will this get rid of stress in your life? No. Only a lifestyle change can do that, but it will make life more tolerable and help you to manage stress more successfully. It's one small change that you can have complete control over. Your body will thank you. Your dog will thank you!

Breathing Exercise

- Take a deep breath into your diaphragm.
- Hold for five seconds.
- Exhale: Release tension and stress.
- Do it again and again, if you desire...

Brief Body Relaxation

- Relax your facial muscles. Take a deep breath.
- Rotate your shoulders forward a few times, then backwards.
- To the count of 10, slowly lift your shoulders up toward your ears. Hold for five seconds; slowly lower to the count of 10 to release upper-body tension.

While you are doing this, say to your dog: "Hey, let's relax for a minute." The dog soon learns that this means "Phew, I'm off the hook for a while, no expectations."

To calm a stressful situation quickly, take a deep breath that goes right down into your diaphragm. If your chest is rising, you are doing it incorrectly. You should feel this deep down in your stomach area (a deep belly breath). Now, try a breathing exercise.

Develop a Sense of Humor!

Humans have been using humor as a survival mechanism since our arms were dragging on the ground. As Lila Green, author of *Making Sense of Humor*, observes, "Those who laugh ... last." Much of this is based on our perspective and attitude. How do you perceive certain situations? For example, most of us would regard aging as a time of reflection and accumulated wisdom. The other side of aging is that our bodies are dete-riorating. Now look at it this way: Growing old is not so bad, especially if you consider the alternative. Get the picture?

Humor prevents hardening of the attitudes when used carefully and in appropriate situations. Here are some other attributes of humor:

• Humor is a common language to which almost everyone can relate.
• Humor is absolutely essential for survival.
• Humor is an instant icebreaker in tense situations.
• Humor relieves stress and nervousness with humor awareness.

Psychologist Rollo May says, "Humor is the healthy way of feeling a distance between one's self and the problem, a way of standing off and looking at the problem with perspective." When we become anxious, our focus becomes narrower and less creative. We are easily angered. Humor is a wonderful coping mechanism, allowing us to cognitively reframe a situation and examine the problem from another viewpoint.

→There are psychological and physical benefits to humor and laughter. A hearty laugh increases the depth of breathing, thus exercis-ing the respiratory muscles.

→Oxygen flows into the blood and is increased, stimulating and benefiting the heart and circulatory system.

→Laughter raises levels of endorphins, which are pain-killing chemicals released by the brain.

→Laughter also reduces pain by distracting attention from it and changing our expectations, thus giving us more mental alertness.

→After you calm down, the pulse rate drops below normal and your skeletal muscles become deeply relaxed. The stress load is lightened.

→The eyes are "the windows of the soul." They brighten and sparkle when we laugh. Have you ever laughed until you cried? Like a good cry, a good giggle releases tears that are cleansing and cathartic.

Life is incongruent and unpredictable. So are puppies and some adult dogs. The next time you feel yourself getting frazzled at a mistake your dog makes, have a humor break. Have a good giggle, then go back to training. Nothing is as bad as it seems a week later. Nothing is worth popping a blood vessel over.

At Dog Talk training classes, we encourage having a good laugh. We have a "hat" theme for graduation. We have been honored with some very creative and clever students. One student glued five pounds of dog kibble onto a straw hat, along with several other doggy objects. It was hysterical, but after 10 minutes in class, she started having the worst headache because the hat weighed a ton. It was an enlightening moment. She was an inspiration because she gracefully laughed about her dilemma, admitting that she "had a ball making the hat with the kids."

We use puppets, stovepipe hats, clown noses, and other silly gadgets. The significance of a "silly" apparatus goes beyond just having a good laugh. It desensitizes the dogs to strange sights and sounds. It gets people to lighten up, thus relaxing the dogs as well.

Family Times and One-on-Ones

Physical: Exercise together and bring the dog(s). Reclarify expectations and goals around financial and physical assets, household chores, and puppy schedules.

Mental: Learn new things together. Share and discuss new training ideas and schedules for the family pets.

Spiritual: Renew commitments. Clarify directions and goals. Pray, worship, meditate, read together, and respect nature.

Social/Emotional: Love and affirm one another. Laugh at "inside jokes" and relax together. Build relationships of trust and unconditional love—relationship skills that you can learn from nature and your dog.

HEALTHY PAWS OF LIFE FOR YOU AND YOUR DOG

There are some habits and frames of mind that have been tested time and again. When integrated as part of our lifestyle and practiced daily, they make life more enjoyable and manageable.

Every day is a brand new adventure, with lessons to be learned. Why not begin your adventure with your dog(s)? If you haven't pawed through Dr. Phillip C. McGraw's books, *Life Strategies: Doing What Works, Doing What Matters* (Hyperion), and *Relationship Rescue: A Seven-Step Strategy for Reconnecting With Your Partner* (Hyperion), we encourage you to do so. Study and absorb his "Ten Laws of Life." These laws apply not only to you, but can easily be adapted to your relationship with your dog. Here are some helpful considerations.

• **Dogs are not disposables or try-ons like shoes.** It makes a heck of lot more sense to get a different pet than to buy one that barks if you don't want to listen to barking. Point taken? If you are a couch potato, before getting a Border Collie that requires continuous mental stimulation and something to herd, research the breed's characteristics. Millions of dogs are available. Take the time to find a like-minded companion.

• **Don't compromise your relationship with your dog over something that won't matter a week from now.** Dogs process information differently than we do, in the here and now. Develop a relationship based on observation and understanding these differences.

• **Dogs (without training or supervision) create their own experiences through guessing, playing and exploring.** Take a walk and find something new to be excited about every day.

• **Accept responsibility and learn from the consequences of your choices.** Every moment counts! When relating to dogs, if something goes awry, refer to your family planner, or creatively make one. You can't control everything in life, but you can control your breath, *so breathe.* Teach your dog to relax!

• **Life rewards actions; actions cure fears.** Remember to train, don't complain; evolve, don't dissolve. Become accountable for what is or isn't happening in your life. Ask yourself, "What is the reward for not changing?" Take action. Get your puppy into a gentle training class.

• **Reality is simply perception and interpretations.** For every ten people (or dogs), there are ten interpretations. Your request to Come may be relevant to you, but not to your dog. Try to put yourself in your dog's place and think about whether you're making it rewarding enough to get the response you're asking for.

• **Life is not always predictable, but it is manageable.** You can take control of your life if you truly want to. Be resilient. Develop healthy coping mechanisms that enable you to bounce back in the face of adversity. Hone up on your life management skills. Become a good listener and observer. Set achievable, flexible goals.

• **Humans and dogs may differ genetically, but when it comes to doing what works, the status quo rules.** The consequence of any behavior, if even remotely satisfactory, will drive human or dog to do it again. A familiar pattern develops, and not necessarily a healthy one, simply one that works. If you identify these behaviors, you can change them.

• **We all use defense (or coping) mechanisms for survival.** We view the world through smoke screens and use what we call "stallers." Some are healthy and protect us; others prevent us from letting go and moving on. Dogs use defense mechanisms for survival and to avoid conflict. Identify the "stallers" in your life — and possibly those in your dog's life.

• **When something feels unfair, then put some integrity back into your life.** Coach family, friends, co-workers and your dogs on how to treat you with respect and reciprocate this gesture.

Owning dogs is a joyful and sometimes humbling experience. Rather than get upset when your dog embarrasses or seems to defy you, take a deep breath, smile, laugh, or apologize. It's over. Later, think about how the situation could be changed.

Acceptance and/or forgiveness are empowering attributes. Open your eyes (and heart) to what anger or resentment might be doing to you and your relationship with your dog. Dogs don't hold grudges. They don't get angry. They use coping mechanisms (fight, flight, freeze, and appease). Forgive yourself for not teaching your dog what, when, where, and for how long. Don't compromise the relationship by wearing "danger, beware of owner" written on your forehead.

We have seen the adversary and it is ourselves! We all have dark shadows. Be your own and your dog's best friend. Step up to the plate with the bat and decide which pitch might be a strike, ball, or home run. Whatever you want, be it more help from your family, a friend to genuinely listen, or your dog to walk by your side rather than lunging, make a list, and shoot for the goals.

Chapter Eighteen

Final Words of Wisdom

In summary, indulge us in making (or repeating) some salient points. The most effective training techniques are the ones that work best for you and your dog. They employ positive, gentle techniques. They teach the meaning and relevance: the whats, what nots, and hows in the most natural and understandable way.

They involve teaching two-way communication. A human learns the language of the dog, while the dog learns the human language. The dog joyfully and without reservation offers us on-the-spot, here-and-now behaviors. If they're not the behaviors we want, then we need to teach the behaviors.

Use an eye of understanding. Through observation, evaluate the results of your training, communication, and relationship with your dog on an ongoing basis. Our friend and fellow trainer, Monique Charbonnier of Gentle Puppy Training in British Columbia, says, "Everyone needs a relationship vacation ... even the dogs." How is your dog responding? Are you communicating clearly and in a way that the dog can understand? Is it realistic? Do you need a "relationship vacation"?

Dogs, like humans, should be evaluated on an individual basis because they're all different. All dogs have a genetic makeup, characteristics, instincts, personalities, and learned behaviors. Some behaviors are learned intentionally while others are inadvertently learned from experiences and associations in life, much as we learn and are influenced by family patterns, beliefs, our culture, and society.

Sage views the world from a different perspective. Dogs, like humans, should
be evaluated on an individual basis because they are all different.
(Photo by Gary Ross)

Allow your dog the time to explore her natural abilities by directing her energy into productive assignments: where to dig, what to chew,
whom to chase, and when to bark or jump. Dogs can be taught discrim-
ination. Their training repertoire is huge. Think about the working dogs
of the world who see and hear for us, search and find, and work in law
enforcement and therapeutic environments.

THINGS WE'VE LEARNED (AND THIS CAN BE READ WITH YOUR DOG IN MIND)

We've learned that:

1. Changing your life starts with changing your mind and attitude. Who you think you are is who you will become. What you think your dog can achieve is usually what he achieves.

2. You teach people and any other species how to treat you! You are accountable for your lives and choices!

3. Knowledge allows you to make informed decisions as you choose pathways in life. You will encounter a vale of tears, laughter, and experiences. Ignorance (blissful or otherwise) is a huge enemy leaving a gaping hole or void, a sense that something is always remiss or missing.

4. You can get by on charm for about 15 minutes. After that, you'd better know something.

5. You shouldn't compare yourself to the best others can do, but to the best *you* can do.

6. It's not what happens to you that's important. It's what you do about it.

7. No matter how thinly you slice it, there are always two sides to reality.

8. You can do something in an instant that can give you heartache for the rest of your life.

9. It's taking you a long time to become the person you want to be.

10. It's a lot easier to react than it is to think proactively.

11. You should always leave loved ones with kind words and a hug. It may be the last time you see them.

12. Either you control your attitude or it controls you.

13. Regardless of how hot and steamy a relationship is at first, the passion fades and there had better be something else to take its place. What you see and hear is truly what you get!

14. Heroes are those people who do what has to be done when it needs to be done, regardless of the consequences.

15. Forgiving takes practice and listening is an art that comes before understanding; understanding comes before wisdom.

16. You can drink lots of water without always carrying a water bottle around.

17. You can get more accomplished without the cell phone glued to your ear!

18. You and your best friend should be able to do anything or nothing and have the best time either way.

19. Sometimes when you're angry you have the right to be angry, but that doesn't give you the right to be cruel *to any species*.

20. True friendship continues to grow, even over the longest distance. The same goes for *true love*. The same goes for *soulmates*.

21. Just because someone doesn't love you the way you want him to doesn't mean he doesn't love you with all he has.

22. No matter how much you care, some people just don't care back.

23. You should never tell a child her dreams are unlikely or outlandish. You should never tell a dog that the hole he dug is disgusting. You should never tell a cat that the dead chipmunk she delivered to you for supper makes you want to hurl. Few things are more humiliating, and what a tragedy it would be if he believed it.

24. No matter how good a friend someone is, he is going to hurt you every once in a while and you must forgive him for that.

25. Stop pretending to do something that you're really never, ever going to do!

26. It isn't always enough to be forgiven by others. Sometimes you have to learn to forgive yourself! You need to let go and get on with it.

27. No matter how badly your heart is broken, the world doesn't stop for your grief.

28. Your background and circumstances may have influenced who you are, but *you are responsible for who you become*.

29. Just because two people argue, it doesn't mean they don't love each other. And just because they don't argue, it doesn't mean they do! Just because your dog misbehaves doesn't mean she is mad at you. And just because she does what you expect doesn't mean she likes it!

30. It takes years to build up trust, and only seconds to destroy it.

31. Two people (or species) can look at the exact same thing and see something completely different.

32. You cannot make someone love you. All you can do is be someone who can be loved.

33. No matter what the consequences, those who have integrity and are fair and honest with themselves get farther in life.

34. Live your life as if you're being videotaped. You never know where it will show up!

35. Be flexible like the healthy branches on a tree. You can bend, but you won't break.

36. Yesterday is history, tomorrow a mystery, and today a gift. That's why we call it "the present." Focus on the "now."

37. Listen to your own intuition, not just your intellect, to rediscover your spirit.

38. Learn something new every day. When you focus your thoughts, they have more power.

39. Respect all living creatures, as they are part of the circle of life; what happens to them, happens to you.

40. The only thing that can create change is change, and change is your choice. Actions cure fears.

41. Lessons are repeated until they are learned.

42. You have spiritual guides and teachers in the universe who are willing to help if you quiet your mind and ask.

43. You must come to experience the unconditional love of a dog and the magic of a child's world!

44. Don't do anything for anyone that you don't feel honestly from the heart. Act with the intent to be fair, have integrity, and be true to yourself, your family, your friends, your dogs, and nature.

45. Learn to create purple snowflakes (imagination) like children do, and wear any darn color you please, whether in vogue or not!!!

46. Learn that you will always be learning.

Recommended Readings

There are many choices in training and behavior books and videos available today. The following is a list of some of the materials that we have found educational, informative, and enjoyable to read. Be mindful that training has revolutionized to being more reward-oriented, using positive reinforcement training techniques. This is pleasurable, reliable, and effective for the owner, trainer, and obviously the dog! All reading is educational, but everyone must develop his or her own style in training. Listen to your common sense, intuition, and heart. Ask yourself, "What feels right ... and what doesn't?" You have choices, so use what works best for you, your family, and your dogs.

TRAINING AND BEHAVIOR

Arden, Andrea. *Dog-Friendly Dog Training*. New York: Howell Book House, 1999.

Beck, Alan, Sc.D. and Katcher, Aaron, M.D. *Between Pets and People*. New York: Putnam, 1983.

Benjamin, Carol Lea. *Dog Problems*. New York: Howell Book House, 1989.

Benjamin, Carol Lea. *Mother Knows Best*. New York: Howell Book House, 1985.

Booth, Sheila. *Purely Positive Training*. Ridgefield, CN: Podium, 1998.

Coren, Stanley, Ph.D. *The Intelligence of Dogs*. New York: The Free Press, 1994.

Donaldson, Jean. *The Culture Clash*. Berkeley: James & Kenneth, 1996.

Dunbar, Dr. Ian. *Dog Behavior*. New York: Howell Book House, 1999.

Dunbar, Dr. Ian. *How to Teach an Old Dog New Tricks*. Berkeley: James & Kenneth, 1996.

Dunbar, Dr. Ian. *Dr. Dunbar's Good Little Dog Book*. Berkeley: James & Kenneth, 1992.

George, Jean Craighead. *How to Talk to Your Dog*. New York: Warner Communications, 1985.

Kilcommons, Brian, and Wilson, Sarah. *Childproofing Your Dog*. New York: Warner Books, 1994.

Kilcommons, Brian, and Wilson, Sarah. *Good Owners, Great Dogs*. New York: Warner Books, 1992.

Knapp, Caroline. *Pack of Two*. New York: Dial Press, 1998.

Laaman, Laura L. *The Dolphin Dynamics*. Franklin Lakes, NJ: Career Press, 1996.

Lorenz, Konrad. *Man Meets Dogs*. New York: Kodansha America, 1994.

Marshall Thomas, Elizabeth. *The Hidden Life of Dogs*. Boston: Houghton Mifflin, 1993.

McElroy, Susan Chernak. *Animals as Teachers & Healers*. New York: Random House, 1998.

The Monks of New Skete. *How to Be Your Dog's Best Friend*. Boston/Toronto: Little, Brown & Co., 1978.

Morris, Desmond. *Dogwatching*. New York: Crown Publishers, 1986.

Moussaieff. Masson, Jeffrey, Ph.D. *Dogs Never Lie about Love*. New York: Three Rivers Press, 1998.

Pryor, Karen. *A Dog and a Dolphin: Introduction to Click & Treat Training*. Waltham, MA: Sunshine, 1995.

Pryor, Karen. *On Behavior: Essays and Research*. Waltham, MA: Sunshine, 1995.

Reid, Pamela J., Ph.D. *Excel-Erated Learning: Explaining How Dogs Learn & How Best to Teach Them*. Berkeley: James Kenneth Publisher, 1996.

Roberts, Monty. *The Man Who Listens to Horses*. New York: Random House, 1997.

Ryan, Terry. *Games People Play ... to Train Their Dogs*. Kula, HI: Legacy By Mail, 1994.

Ryan, Terry. *Life Beyond Block Healing*. Kula, HI: Legacy by Mail, 1996.

Rugaas, Turid. *On Talking Terms with Dogs: Calming Signals*. Kula, HI: Legacy by Mail, 1997.

Volhard, Jack and Bartlett, Melissa. *What All Good Dogs Should Know*. New York: Howell Book House, 1991.

PET-ASSISTED THERAPY

Burch, Mary, Ph.D. *Volunteering with Your Pet*. New York: Howell Book House, 1996.

Delta Society/Pet Partners. *Pet/Parners Manual*. Renton, WA: Delta Society, 1996.

Root, Jacqueline P. *K-9 Therapy Group*. Fairfax, VA: Denlinger, 1990.

Ruckert, Jane. *The Four-Footed Therapist*. Berkeley: Ten Speed Press, 1987.

SELF-HELP / PSYCHOLOGY

Bowles, Robert C. *Learning, Motivation & Cognition*. Washington, D.C.: American Psychological Press, 1997.

Brandon, Nathaniel, Ph.D. *The Six Pillars of Self Esteem*. New York: Bantam Books, 1994.

Carlson, Richard, Ph.D. *Don't Sweat the Small Stuff and It's All Small Stuff*. New York: Hyperion, 1997.

Christian, Sandy, M.S.W., and Tubesing, Nancy Loving. *Instant Icebreakers: High Impact Learning*. Duluth, MN: Whole Person Associates, 1997.

Covey, Stephen R. *The 7 Habits of Highly Effective Families*. New York: Golden Books, 1997.

DeBono, Edward. *Serious Creativity*. New York: Harper Collins, 1993.

Donaldson, Michael and Donaldson, Mimi. *Negotiating For Dummies*. New York: Hungry Minds Inc., 1996.

Goodheart, Annette, Ph.D. *Laughter Therapy*. Beachwood, OH: Wellness Reproductions, 1994.

London, Joan. *A Bend in the Road Is Not the End of the Road*. New York: William Morrow & Co., 1998.

McGraw, Phillip C., Ph.D. *Life Strategies: Doing What Works, Doing What Counts*. New York: Hyperion, 1999.

McGraw, Phillip C., Ph.D. *Relationship Rescue*. New York: Hyperion, 2000.

Shinberg, Elaine Fantle. *Blended Families*. New York: Berkley Books, 1999.

Tolle, Eckhart. *The Power of Now*. Novato, CA: New World Library, 1999.

Winfrey, Oprah. *Make the Connection*. New York: Hyperion, 1996.

HEALTH

Aiello, Susan, and May, Asa, eds. *The Merck Veterinary Manual, Eighth Edition*. Rahway, NJ: Merck Publishing Group, 1998.

Carlson, Delbert, D.V.M., and Griffin, James, M.D. *Dog Owner's Home Veterinary Handbook*. New York: Howell Book House, 1992.

Tellington-Jones, Linda. *The Tellington Touch: A Breakthrough Technique to Train & Care for Your Favorite Animal*. Santa Fe: Viking, 1992.

Volhard, Wendy, and Brown, Kerry L., D.V.M.. *The Holistic Guide for a Healthy Dog*. New York: Howell Book House, 1995.

Index

About the Authors

Maureen and Gary Ross study behavior, training, learning patterns and paradigms for dogs and other species — especially wolves. They have been walking-the-walk and learning to talk to dogs (and to their families) for more years then they care to mention.

Co-founders of Dog Talk and TheraPet (established 1989 and 1998, respectively), the Rosses are dedicated to the enhancement of human-canine relationships by specifically targeting families and focusing on interactive team training and relationship. Dog Talk offers basic and intermediate education and training, behavioral counseling, and specialized training in pet-facilitated therapy and humor development.

As licensed team evaluators and pet partner team instructors for Delta Society, they are active in canine, feline, equine, and alternative forms of pet-assisted therapies. They present workshops for health-care professionals and volunteers at universities, hospitals, health-care facilities, and conferences.

Both are charter members (and presenters) of the Association of Pet Dog Trainers (APDT) and belong to the National Association of Dog Obedience Instructors (NADOI), Delta Society, and various breed clubs.